Praise for *Seven Lives*

"There is an appreciation of life, but there is also directness and acceptance of good and bad—the struggles are played out in the same calm, observant tone as the pleasures. Perhaps it is because the narrator leaves the judgment to God or to providence—and simply records."

—DEBORAH E. RYEL
ASSOCIATE PROFESSOR EMERITA
COLLEGE OF DU PAGE, GLEN ELLYN, ILLINOIS

"In *Seven Lives*, Solveig Sedlet describes her charming Danish village and the rich characters of her family and neighbors. From them she learns values and work habits that she must use to deal with future tough challenges, the German occupation, working in England, moving to the United States, marriage, widowhood, and raising four children. I was fortunate to discuss the book with Solveig. She is an honest and resourceful person and the book reflects these qualities."

—ROBERT E. ARTHUR, PH.D.
PROFESSOR OF PSYCHOLOGY
UNIVERSITY OF WISCONSIN-LA CROSSE

"You took me in time and place to your hometown. In my mind's eye, I could visualize the buildings and the people."

—SAM SATO, WRITER
HAWAII

"I can almost imagine a Hollywood set director working straight from your piece without any difficulty."

—TOM TIPTON
ASSOCIATE PROFESSOR OF ENGLISH
COLLEGE OF DU PAGE, GLEN ELLYN, ILLINOIS

"[Solveig's poems] stand as such stark disclosures of the heart's deepest cries that I think they are universal."

—LAURA ANSCHICKS
PROFESSOR EMERITA OF ENGLISH
COLLEGE OF DU PAGE, GLEN ELLYN, ILLINOIS

My
Seven
Lives

Solveig Sedlet

faith
hope
charity

Cover and interior designed by Sue Knopf, Graffolio.

Printed in the United States of America.

ISBN 10: 0-9766437-0-7
ISBN 13: 978-0-9766437-0-8

Distributed by:

Skandisk, Inc.
6667 West Old Shakopee Rd., Suite 109
Bloomington, MN 55438-2622

Tel. 1-800-468-2424 (or 952-829-8998)
www.skandisk.com

To Jake

1 Childhood   1

Stories from Fjelstrup:
A Magical Childhood in Denmark

2 Five Bitter Years   75

Living under German Occupation

3 Venturing Away   109

A New Life Away from Denmark

4 Transatlantic   131

Coming to America

5 Widowhood   145

A Year in Denmark

6 New Beginnings   171

An End to Loneliness

7 John   217

A Troubled Soul

PREFACE

Through the years that it has taken me to write these tales, I have often been asked, "Do you ever find you have nothing to write about?"

Without hesitation my answer has always been, "No. Never." In attending writing classes at the Iowa Summer Writing Festival at the University of Iowa and the Wisconsin University Writing Camp in Rhinelander, and at varied classes at the College of Du Page, Illinois, it has often occurred to me that keeping a record is important. By writing about the experiences I have lived through, some very good, some very bad, I can leave a record for future generations. I hope these stories from a multifaceted life will interest my children and my grandchildren, who can tell their own children about their great-grandmother, who followed the millions of other immigrants coming to America.

I arrived in New York on a Swedish boat on a cold winter's day in 1949. I left an old life and started a new one. All told, I have lived seven lives, each so different, each a part of who I am.

—Solveig Sedlet

Life

The web of our life is of a mingled yarn,
good and ill together.

All's Well That Ends Well
WILLIAM SHAKESPEARE

All the world's a stage
and all the men and women merely players;
They have their exits and their entrances,
And one man in his time plays many parts,
his acts being seven ages.

As You Like It
WILLIAM SHAKESPEARE

Denmark

Fjelstrup, Denmark, circa 1935.

1

CHILDHOOD

Stories from Fjelstrup:
A Magical Childhood in Denmark

The Sound of Church Bells, Enduring Forever

I am going to tell a lot of stories about my family, and about the home we made in our small village, and about the people there who made it so memorable a childhood. I want to capture for the reader the nuances of the place and the people; they are so vivid in me still.

I want to convey the innocence, the bare, raw emotions, and also the playfulness and loyalty that existed in a community of fewer than five hundred people. Such was my hometown, Fjelstrup, Denmark.

How to tie these stories together? To find what is common in them all, and to give a sense of the flow of time?

*As I looked back again and again, it finally occurred to me that through all the years, filled with events both happy and tragic, through wars and Depression years, through unavoidable disasters and times of oppression, there was one steady, ever-predictable denominator, a recurring daily event that never failed, not ever: **The sound of the church bells.***

From the high towers of the old church that sits squarely in the middle of town, one can hear the bells every day at sunrise, and again when the day is done. For five minutes they ring out over the fields and housetops, and always at the end comes the sound of three bells rung three times, representing the holy Trinity, to remind us of God's presence.

The sound of the bells is so much a part of the lives of the townfolks, most of the time they hardly hear it. Still, that sound is an important part of the structure of their lives. I can just hear them say, We had better get started, the bells rang five minutes ago. Or, Hurry along children, you'll be late for school; didn't you hear the bells?

In the evening, men gather their tools and head for home at the sound of the bells, and the mothers call their children and put supper on the table.

When someone dies, the bells sound at mid-morning, and the flags are lowered to half-mast to honor the departed. On holy days like Easter and Christmas, the big bell is joined by a smaller, rarely used bell, and they chime in joyful unison.

The only other time both of these bells chimed together (for one whole joyful hour!) was when the second world war ended and our country was once again free.

The bells of Fjelstrup brought pattern and order to our existence. Now, thousands of miles and many years away, I find it reassuring to know that they continue to shape the days of those who still live, and those who will live, in my hometown.

Fjelstrup church.

Introducing My Village, My Family, My Childhood

Let me tell you about my small village of about five hundred souls in the southern part of Denmark called South Jutland *(Sønderjylland)*, where I was born in 1925. I am not talking about the way it is there now, with all the fancy sidewalks and streetlights, with names for all the streets and numbers on the houses.

I am talking about the way it was when I was a small child, when I was growing up among people who now lie tucked away with their memories, inside the sturdy stone wall that surrounds the big white church in the middle of town. Those folks raised their children, plied their trades, and worked their farms in a place so small one could pass through with hardly a notice. But I have not forgotten those people, and I hope my stories will help you see them through my eyes. I want you to know them.

The main street through Fjelstrup used to be a narrow roadway winding its way by the west side of the church. Most things of importance went on along this street. Besides the church, there were the schoolhouse, and the big, clumsy railroad station, and a number of shops, businesses, and houses. As the village grew, all those twists and turns must have become too difficult to deal with; the decision was made to build a new road straight through town on the other side, to the east of the church. This happened sometime around 1923, before I was born.

The old road became known simply as *Gammelvej* (Old-way), and the new road become *Nyvej* (New-way). People then didn't name streets and roads the way we do today. There were no traffic lights or stop signs to slow traffic. I suppose if one did not have business in Fjelstrup, there was not much reason to stop.

The whole corner where New-way and North-way intersect was occupied by my father's family. On the northeast corner sits what is still called *Fjelstrup Kro & Gæstgivergård* (Fjelstrup Inn and Guest House). The inn is much like many scattered all over Denmark, but this one is special, because it was my home. It was my whole world, really, with my mother,

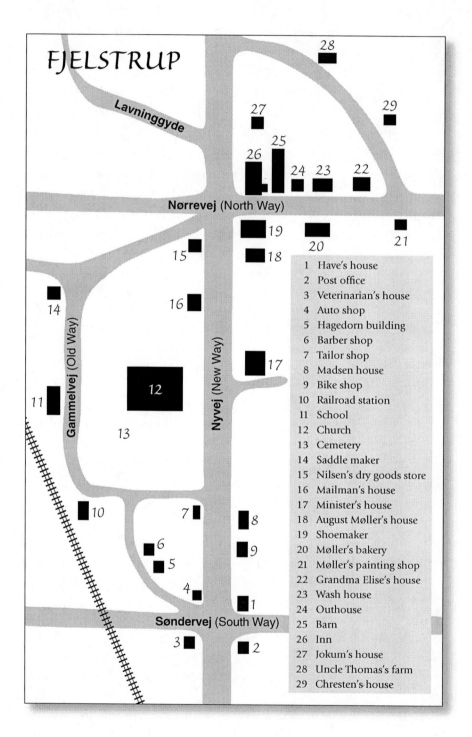

FJELSTRUP

Lavninggyde

Nørrevej (North Way)

Gammelvej (Old Way)

Nyvej (New Way)

Søndervej (South Way)

1 Have's house
2 Post office
3 Veterinarian's house
4 Auto shop
5 Hagedorn building
6 Barber shop
7 Tailor shop
8 Madsen house
9 Bike shop
10 Railroad station
11 School
12 Church
13 Cemetery
14 Saddle maker
15 Nilsen's dry goods store
16 Mailman's house
17 Minister's house
18 August Møller's house
19 Shoemaker
20 Møller's bakery
21 Møller's painting shop
22 Grandma Elise's house
23 Wash house
24 Outhouse
25 Barn
26 Inn
27 Jokum's house
28 Uncle Thomas's farm
29 Chresten's house

father, and two siblings, Gerda and Willy, respectively two and four years older than I. All of us children were born in the bedroom upstairs.

The only thing I was ever told about my birth was that I arrived in the afternoon of a busy day when there was a big funeral coffee going on downstairs. To this day, people gather at the inn after a church service to memorialize the departed with speeches and songs, and of course lots of coffee and fancy cakes. On that February day of my birth, Grandmother Elise was put in charge downstairs while the midwife helped my mother upstairs. My mother told me that I was a longer baby than my siblings, and she had trouble getting the receiving blanket to cover my feet! I guess it follows that I also grew taller than either my sister or brother and, indeed, my parents. Yet I am only a bit over 5'5".

The inn was built in 1846. It was old and impractical. Originally it was a retirement home for a minister, I was told, and it was my grandfather, Søren Wilhelm Petersen, who converted it to an inn and the adjoining grocery and farm supply store.

We lived in the inn and restaurant. The restaurant had five tables with red and white checked tablecloths—Danish colors, of course. The four windows were hung with lace curtains, and my mother kept potted

plants on the sills. The room was heated by a beautiful, large, floor-to-ceiling-type stove called a Kakkelown. It was decorated with ornate light green tiles. Behind a counter there was a tall wooden cabinet that held different kinds of glasses and lovely small cups for coffee punches.

The inn as it looked when I was a child.

The inn as it looks today.

In the middle of it there was a small cabinet with a glass door, where cigars and cigarettes were kept.

The most unusual feature of the restaurant was the ceiling. Inside two large circles, angels had been painted. On quiet days when no one was in the room, I liked to lie on the floor and gape at those angels floating on white clouds in the painted blue sky above me. They must have been left over from the time when the minister lived there.

The pious pictures did not seem to inhibit the brawling beer drinkers or the noisy card players. My father installed a radio-record player next to the counter, and when a young couple stopped in for their evening coffee, I was sometimes asked to change the records to make a more romantic setting.

The floor was made of wide, dark brown oak boards. My mother or the maid polished them with paste wax and shined them with a heavy, long-handled polishing brush. It was a terrible job to get the shine back after a big party when people had dragged in dirt and spilled beer.

Behind the counter, a swinging door led into a large kitchen where our mother and the maid did all the cooking on a woodstove. I vaguely remember a long kitchen cabinet being installed under the windows and my mother's happiness with the added storage space. As in most homes, the kitchen was the center of activity and fun.

We took our meals in an everyday room *(daglig stue)* right next to the kitchen. At the table where we ate, we also did our homework, played games, and did projects. Our father had his desk and his radio in one corner, and it was absolute law that we could not talk or even whisper while he listened to the seven o'clock news.

Grandma's house.

Toward the street there was a fancy parlor, seldom used, with furniture upholstered in red velvet. We had our great Christmas dinner in there, but two days later, when different organizations and clubs held their Christmas parties, we had to vacate the parlor so that people could walk through it into the dance hall.

In the backyard you would have found a barn and around a dozen pigs, seven cows, and two horses; a chicken house, a wash house, and of course, the outhouse. For a small girl, here were all the trappings one could ever want, right within reach. It was an important part of the setting for what I have come to call a magical childhood.

Since my father's family essentially filled that whole corner of New-way and North-way, we truly lived in one another's backyards. Uncle Jokum, Father's older brother, ran the grocery and farm supply store attached to the inn. He lived with his wife, Marie, and two children, Elise and William, about two hundred yards to the north, in a fancy gray brick house. Halfway between Jokum's house and the inn was a pump, the only water source for both households. All the water had to be carried into the houses in buckets. Having only this one pump as the sole supply of water did at times cause some friction between the families. I will explain more about this later on.

The seven of us cousins: Egon, William, Willy, Gerda, Solveig, Lisse, Elise.

At the east end of the attached dance hall was our garden, with flowers and fruit trees and Grandmother's four beehives, and just beyond it was Grandmother's house. My grandfather Søren Wilhelm had that house built when my parents took over the inn in 1920. It was a pretty house with lots of gingerbread, gables and dormers, and a balcony on the second floor. Living so close, grandfather kept his hand in all transactions and worked as the bookkeeper. I was often told that he was a kind, soft-spoken man, but he died before I could know him.

Father's sister, Aunt Hanne, and her husband, Herman Rohard, lived in the apartment above Grandmother Elise. Like Jokum and Marie, they had two children. They were named Lisse and Egon. Herman had been born in Germany, and all his life he spoke with an accent. He did not work in the family business, but had a job in the grain depository in town. In her youth, Aunt Hanne was considered to be the village beauty. Her hair fell in thick brown curls around her pretty face. She was slim and delicate, but marred by a hip deformity that her mother had refused to have fixed when she was a child. She said she could not bear to put her beautiful baby in a plaster cast.

Hanne was a gifted pianist and used her skill to supplement Herman's meager income. She gave lessons, and she played for dances

Father, Gerda, Willy, Mother, and me (Solveig).

in all the nearby meeting halls as well as at many functions at the inn. She accompanied the silent movies when they were shown once a month.

So here we were: three families with seven children, all born within six years, and Grandmother Elise to keep an eye on all of us. It was a wonderful place and time to be a child, and I have countless memories and stories to tell.

Fun in a Country Inn—1930

Life at the inn was very different from that in the other homes around us. It was a busy place, with many people coming and going. There were meetings and dances, weddings and funerals, and once every month the movie-man came with his big black case. The case held the projector and a smaller case for reels. Two holes had been cut through the wall in our small sitting room adjoining the big hall. The small hole was for the man to peek through, and the larger was for the lens of the projector. He set the whole thing up during the afternoon, and in the evening people came to watch the silent movie on our big screen. Our Aunt Hanne accompanied the action on the piano.

I have no memory of the films that were shown, just a vague impression of some political filmstrips showing poor, overworked, suppressed people being pushed around.

My sister, Gerda, and I were the envy of our school friends because we were right there in the center of all this activity. One of our very favorite things was to sit upstairs in the gallery overlooking the dance hall. Our observations from that roost provided much of the information we shared at school. Sitting on the floor behind the banister, we could peek between the boards and see young people from the farms and nearby towns flirting with one another. People from many neighboring communities came to these dances, some of them from as far away as Christiansfeld, about five miles. This was before anyone had cars; they either had to walk or bike to get to Fjelstrup. No one from Haderslev, eleven kilometers away, ever came.

I do remember the tension caused by the brothers Scønneman, from Christiansfeld. They were drinkers and brawlers, and word got around quickly whenever they arrived, so my father kept a close tab on their beer intake. Sometimes a fight broke out and we worried about our dad getting hurt, but Gerda and I were safe up in the balcony.

Aunt Hanne and a dour looking violinist called Mr. Tygesen provided the music. Sound equipment did not yet exist, so certainly no one had to suffer from busted eardrums. The girls sat around the dance floor talking and gossiping and admiring each other's hairdos and dresses while the guys stood in the usual cluster by the entrance door.

Before the music started, my father came in with a tray of shaved wax flakes and spread them all over the dancing area to make it smooth and easy to glide over. Some of those farm boys needed all the help they could get.

Gerda and I were allowed to watch the dancing until nine o'clock. There were no lights in the gallery, so we could just sit there unseen, whispering. We speculated on who was dating whom, and who was new in town, and where had so-and-so come from? We argued over which girl was the prettiest and who was the handsomest guy or the best dancer. Even after our mother came to herd us to bed, we still had a first class view of the action, because our bedroom window was directly over the entrance door to the inn. After

Mother had kissed us good night, we sneaked out of bed and hung on our elbows in the windowsill, watching people coming and going. We saw lots of hugging and kissing, and we kept close track of the blossoming romances—all of which we could relate in school the next day!

All was not sweetness and light. Sometimes those young men argued, and after a long night of sweating and drinking beer, where did they go to settle the score? Right beneath our bedroom window!

Gerda and I categorized the many kinds of fights. There were drunken fights, where no one got hurt too much because they couldn't balance after all the drinking. Then there were jealousy fights that never seemed to amount to much unless the girl in question was watching (she usually wasn't). There were real drunken brawls, though, too: mean, angry fights with crowds of cheering drunks egging the combatants on. Usually those fights involved the Scønneman brothers. When our father and some other men came to stop them, we got scared and hid under our bedcovers.

Did we learn something from all this? I think we did. We learned about human nature: vanity, love and hate, and the effects of alcohol. We also learned that after the party was over and the new day came, all was well and peace was restored.

Until the next gathering!

Family Ways

In our village and in our home, life ran along in predictable patterns, giving us a sense of belonging and the comfort of habits. My parents each had responsibilities that were accomplished with much hard work and cooperation. Along with the farmland and tending the animals, besides running the inn, they found time to give us three kids good values and abundant love.

Each had a helper. Father had a young farmhand, and Mother had a very able maid. Remember, too, that Grandmother Elise, the matriarch, lived close by in her house at the end of our garden, and she had a keen eye for what was going on. Indeed, the whole clan, occupying a good-sized triangle in the village, lived within five hundred feet of one another.

Grandma and Hanne hold Lisse.

In such a tight nucleus, there was, of course, some friction. Family members were sometimes pricked with envy, one-upmanship and pettiness. We children were aware of the mother-daughter gossip between Grandmother Elise and Aunt Hanne, for example, and we knew that sometimes it hurt our mother. Grandmother had her preferences within the family, and we knew that Aunt Hanne's two kids, Lisse and Egon, were her favorites. I can remember times she made doll clothes for Lisse but not for Gerda and me, and I felt sad about it, but we just had to live with the disappointment.

Even though she was of small stature, Grandmother Elise was a formidable lady. She demanded absolute respect, and she never demonstrated affection with hugs and kisses. The memory of our Sunday ritual with Grandmother still amuses me.

First, on Saturday afternoon, Gerda and I had to go over and invite her for Sunday dinner. We were told to say, quite formally, "Grandmother, our mother sent us to invite you for dinner tomorrow." Nine times out of ten we were sent home with the message that she would be pleased to come. Once in a great while, though, she would say, in a haughty way, "Tell your

Grandfather Søren
Wilhelm Petersen.

Grandmothers Elise
Petersen and Anne
Sofie Ahrenkiel.

mother that I have been invited to your Uncle Jokum's house and I can't come this Sunday."

I'm not sure how much this bothered my mother, but we all knew that Grandmother catered to Jokum even though he ignored her most of the time. It was also clear that she was very cool to Aunt Marie.

When she did agree to come to our house, the final part of the ritual came on Sunday. At exactly 11:45 A.M. we had to go over and get her and escort her to our house. I don't remember her ever giving Mother a hand, but of course we had Maggie, our good maid. Right after dinner, Grandmother returned to her own house to nap.

She did often get involved at the inn, though. She enjoyed helping with big parties and dances, being a part of the action, and dealing with customers. In this way she was a resource to our mother.

*Jokum, Elise
and Marie on
a bicycle in
Kolding.*

Later in my life I wondered how she spent her days. Family members
came and went throughout the day, and if somebody did not show up
for several days, we heard about it. Whenever we dropped in on her,
she would be sitting at the kitchen table reading her magazines. I don't
remember any books. Usually she was happy to see us, and she put us to
work grinding coffee beans for her evening and morning coffee. We held
the mill in our laps. She had a set of binoculars right next to her chair,
and when she saw someone coming down the road, she peered at them
through those glasses. She took notice of what people wore, and she
speculated on where they might be going. Without moving from her little
kitchen perch, she somehow knew everything that went on in town. As we
grew older and started going to dances, she managed to find out who took
us home and what went on at the dance. In this way, she kept us in line;
we did not want her disapproval.

After I left the village, I never received a letter from her, nor did I write
to her, but when I went back, one of the first things I always had to do was
visit her. She died in 1955, while my parents were visiting me in St. Louis.
Although she had been sick for a long time, she had encouraged them to
go. Some days after Aunt Hanne's letter came telling us the sad news, my
parents got dressed up and walked to the nearby Lutheran church and
said prayers for her. I stayed home with my baby Karen.

Aunt Marie, Uncle Jokum's wife, was capable of vindictiveness. One day, she had her maid pump the well dry, even though she knew that it was Mother's big laundry day. I don't know what set her off; I doubt if anyone knew except her. When my father got wind of it, he ran across the yard to her house and overturned all the big tubs and buckets in which she had stored water. I still remember seeing the gallons and gallons of water running over the doorsill into the yard. I looked at my father with awe and renewed respect. I don't believe that Marie ever did anything like that again. She was troublesome as a neighbor, but she was part of the family, and, living so close, we all had to learn to get along, and we did. In fact, I marvel that it went as well as it did. Two factors made it possible. One was the measured courtesy and respect for privacy, shown most of the time. The other all-important factor was the total devotion, love, and commitment between my parents.

Father taught us table manners and respect for our elders. He taught us the value of reading and learning. As we followed him around in his daily routines, he found time to explain how things worked, and to instruct us. I spent many hours watching him take the motor apart in our Model T Ford while he carefully explained what made it run.

He told me about stars and the northern lights that flashed on winter nights. He told me why crops had to be rotated in the fields, and that the meadowlark was the only bird that could sing while flying high. He was always interesting. When it was possible, he took me along to the big windmill, where wheat and barley were ground into food for the pigs and horses and into flour for the household, and he took me to the blacksmith to have the horses shod. He even had me holding onto his pants legs while he plowed, furrow after furrow. His work was constant and hard, but he found time to talk to me while he did his chores.

Mother was the nurturer, the hostess of the inn, the organizer and cook. Her hours were long, too, but by watching her we learned countless skills such as bread baking and preserving fruits, vegetables, eggs and meats. We learned to knit and sew and to be resourceful and independent.

Only once did I hear my parents argue, loud and angry, and I feared my whole world would split apart. They disciplined us with love, trust, and high expectations. I will always be grateful to them. Material things were scarce, but love was abundant in our house.

Neighbor Folks

As I have mentioned, the whole northeast corner of New-way and North-way was occupied by our family, with aunts, uncles, cousins, and Grandmother Elise all living in a cluster only a few hundred feet apart.

On the other three corners of the crossroads were Marie Bramsen's house, Andreas Nielsen's dry goods store, and Magnus Olsen's shoemaker shop. I'll tell you about these people in time, but first let's go down the road about fifty yards to Møller's bakery. It was truly a place of wonder for my sister and me.

I never knew the old baker, but his wife, Granny Møller, always sat in a chair in the kitchen. I never spoke with her, but it seemed she sat there for years, usually doing something with her hands, like peeling potatoes or apples, or knitting socks with her four needles going round and round with great speed. I don't remember her dying, but where else would she have gone?! In her day she must have been quite a woman. She gave birth to four sons in the upstairs bedroom, and in time she hauled them, one by one, over to the church to have them named.

All my life I have wondered how she thought up those names. The first she called Andor. Unusual, but not too bad. The next was August. And the third was Ferdinand! In Fjelstrup, Denmark!

Delivery wagon.

Her lively imagination must have run out of steam then, because the fourth one she called simply Hans. How dull, especially since he grew up to fancy himself an artist. He did not join the family business, but instead set up shop as a house painter a little farther down the road. He was always known as Painter-master Møller. Even on the brown granite marker on his grave it says, *Painter-master Hans Møller!* In fact, the people who worked for him were just painters. He was what one in those days called a dandy, always immaculately dressed, and in his spare time he dabbled in the art

The bakery brothers: August, Andor, and Ferdinand Møller.

of painting with oils. He hung a lot of them around his shop. I had plenty of time to study them while he and my father were settling world affairs, but even as a very small girl, maybe five or six years old, I was unimpressed with the pink sunsets and gloomy pine forests. Gerda and I made up names we thought more fitting for Hans, like Phillipe or Jacques.

Andor eventually took over the bakery, and August and Ferdinand worked with him. Each had his own table in the bakery where he did his particular job. Andor made all the bread and rolls. Next to his station was a big drum-like bread mixer where he made the dough for the hard rye bread that is eaten all over Denmark. I never saw the mixer running because Andor got up between three and four in the morning to get things started so that bread would be ready for morning delivery. (The delivery man's name was Gerhard Skovlund, and much was said about his charming ways with the housewives!) I did see Andor make the hard-crusted rolls, though, and I was quite impressed with the speed with which he could make two rolls at the same time, one in each hand. I loved those hard rolls, but we got them only on Sundays. Andor was a short roly-poly man with an air of authority, and for many years he served as mayor of Fjelstrup.

On a long table under the window August did his job. He was tall, skinny, and very gentle, and I suppose he must have had some artistic abilities too, for he created all the fancy cakes and tortes. He had tall containers filled with jellies and jams used between the many layers of cake. He made custard every day and he whipped cream by hand in a big round bowl held in the crook of his arm. It was the best thing in the world to see him decorate those fancy cakes with lovely flowers and shapes fashioned from colored marzipan. Sometimes he wrote names or appropriate messages on the cakes, using red jelly, things like *Congratulations on Your Wedding Day (Bryllupsdag)* or perhaps *Happy Birthday (Til Lykke med Fødselsdagen)*. When he made napoleons he let us eat the crumbs left at the ends, and when the pouch of whipping cream was almost empty, he squirted dollops on the backs of our hands and we licked it with our fingers.

Ferdinand was the cookie maker and all-round helper. His table was next to the big ovens that were built into the walls. He kept an eye on things that were baking. He was small and quiet and sickly, and did not talk much, but he too was gentle and kind. He never married, and in later years he became the bookkeeper at the town office. He lived in the house with August, and one room in the house was his office.

August was also a long-time bachelor, but that ended when a woman named Tinne swept into town. After she had spotted August and decided that he should marry her, there were no more bachelor days for him. She was a strong-willed woman and didn't quite seem to fit in, but she kept her house and garden neat as a pin, so the housewives accepted her. She ran a tight ship, and it was her idea to move the village office into their house. She charged the township good money for the space and she charged for Ferdinand's lodgings.

It took some years before she and August had children. I believe she had one or more miscarriages. When they finally had their son, Peter, the whole town rejoiced, and as was the custom, the flags were raised at all the houses. I very clearly remember August coming to our back door early one morning. He knocked softly, and when I opened the door, there he was with his jacket over his long baker's apron. He spoke quietly and his eyes filled with tears as he said, "Solveig, will you tell your mother that we had a little son this morning." He looked cold and tired and happy, and even though I knew him so well, I couldn't think of a single thing to say.

Tinne paraded Peter up and down the street in his stroller, showing him off to neighbors. He became a chubby toddler with soft white-blond hair that stuck straight up in the air like a baby's brush. Every day he pedaled down around the corner to meet his father as he came walking home for noon dinner. Peter got a little spoiled, of course; it was hard to say who loved him the most, Tinne, August, or old Uncle Ferdinand.

Andor, the Baker-master, and his wife, Didde, had two children: Fritz, who was Gerda's age, two years older than I, and a little girl called Lisbet. When the polio epidemic went through the country in the thirties, Lisbet, who was a spindly child (my mother said she ate too much cake), was infected. She was sick for a long time, and she lost the use of one arm.

Today, the bakery, once so busy, has mostly succumbed to the large supermarkets of nearby Haderslev. It is still in business, although the ovens are not in use every day anymore, and all of the Møller family is gone now.

Uncle Thomas Ahrenkiel's farm.

The Farms around Us

Around the nucleus of the small village of Fjelstrup were many farms, scattered around the gently rolling countryside. Down *Søndervej* (South-way) and *Nørrevej* (North-way) and all the small interconnecting country lanes lay lovely old homesteads that in many cases had been occupied by members of the same families for hundreds of years.

The farmers came to town to get supplies at the grocery stores and to sell their harvest yields of wheat and oats and barley. They came to have their shoes fixed and their clothes made and to have harnesses for the horses repaired. On Sundays some of them came to church, and in time they brought their loved ones to the family plot in the cemetery inside the old stone wall beneath the white tower. Afterwards they came to our family inn to drink coffee and reminisce under the thick haze of their cigar smoke. Mostly, though, they lived their lives on their farms, each of which was like its own small community. Activities were governed by the seasons. Spring and summer were, of course, the busiest. Fall led into a more relaxed time when farmers could catch up on indoor repairs and other necessary activities.

Cousin Lisse Schultz's farm.

Most of the old Danish farms were built in pretty much the same style. Four large buildings formed a square with a courtyard in the center, protected from the wind. The main building was living quarters, occupied by the family and by the maids, who had rooms in the loft. Usually there were two entrance doors, one used mostly for company and one for everyday use. The everyday door was near the kitchen and the big room where the farmhands took their meals and spent their time in the evenings. The family had its own dining room, sometimes shared with the maids.

Another building was for the cow barn and horse stable. Since I am writing about the period from 1925 to 1940, tractors had not come into use. Most farms had at least four horses. Sometimes an additional, lighter, more elegant horse was used to pull the farmer's hansom carriage. The farmhands, usually two or three of them, had their rooms above the horse stable. They fed and cared for their four-legged neighbors below. To this day I wonder how those young men managed to keep even halfway clean up there in their unheated, damp rooms. They had no toilet facilities except for the common outhouse, and of course they had no running water—neither hot nor cold. None of us did until years later. They were supplied with a small washstand, a cake of soap, and one towel a week.

Only when they had to go to something special did they ask for a kettle of hot water with which to wash and shave.

The married livestock keeper looked after the twenty or so cows. He and his family were housed in a small cottage nearby that belonged to the farm; his job was often a lifelong occupation. He would raise his children in the small house and work his grueling hours. Generally, he was looked upon as a well-respected citizen in town. His days started at 5 A.M. with the first milking, all of it done by hand of course, since milking machines had not yet been invented. His wife was expected to help him get the job done before the jugs were picked up by the dairy wagon at seven. When cows were calving, he often spent the night in the barn, watching over a newborn calf. He also had to feed and care for the pigs, which were housed in the second building across the courtyard. He had to clean stalls and likewise take the role of midwife when a sow was birthing. A good-sized farm usually had between fifteen and twenty-five pigs. It was a hard life, but if the livestock keeper was conscientious and trustworthy, he was fairly well paid.

The fourth building, where the large entrance into the courtyard was located, was the place where all the straw, hay, wheat, barley, and oats used for feeding the animals were stored. Out back were the chicken house and yard and a shed or two for storing the farm implements such as plows and harrows. And of course, there was the outhouse.

Since most raw materials were at hand, a farm was mostly self-sufficient. The wheat used for baking was taken to the mill and ground, as were oats and barley for the animals. Several times a year a pig was slaughtered for meat, and a large vegetable garden provided most of the produce. Potatoes, a mainstay in the Danish diet, were grown in a field large enough to yield a supply that would last through the winter. They were stored in a root cellar along with carrots and apples. Of course, eggs were plentiful, and when hens aged beyond their laying days, they became Sunday's chicken dinner.

Now, cooking a chicken sounds easy, but in those days, getting it ready to cook was no small matter. First the old hen's head was chopped off on a block and left to bleed while water was heated for scalding. Next the carcass was dipped into the boiling water so that its feathers came off easily, and then it had to be singed over a hot flame to remove the last hairs, and the innards had to be removed. If done carefully, this latter task was easy, but it took some practice not to cut into the intestine. The heart, liver, and gizzard were saved for soup, and finally, the chicken was ready to cook. With so many to feed, it took three or four chickens, so the job had to be started in the early morning if dinner was going to be ready at noon, when it was always served.

Maybe this kind of life seems like endless drudgery, with hardly any time or energy left for anything but work and sleep. In fact, there was time for leisure, too, and there was a great camaraderie among the young people. When they gathered, there was much laughter and singing. Each small town had its own meeting hall *(forsamlingshus)*, easily reached on a bicycle, and many kinds of activities went on there, including gymnastics, folk dancing, handball, and soccer.

Most popular, however, were the dances. Gerda and I were not allowed to go until we were sixteen. How we looked forward to that time! We primped and preened in front of the mirror, and we always wore skirts or dresses, usually homemade. There were no jeans in those days.

The boys gathered in a herd in front of the door, eyeing the girls who were sitting against the wall on a line of benches opposite the door and the boys. A few local talents usually supplied the music: a piano, a fiddle, maybe an accordion, all played as well as could be managed. My brother, Willy, played the accordion well, and in his teens he formed a group with a couple of his buddies to play at the dances.

Once the music started, the idea was for a guy to get across the floor and ask a pretty girl to dance. Some of those farm guys were pretty good dancers. Where they learned it I can't imagine, but most of them could do a fox-trot or the waltz well enough. The ones who couldn't dance were avoided like the plague!

When the dance was over, the girl was returned to her bench, and the whole ritual was repeated again and again, all night long. The big challenge to a boy was to capture the girl of his choice for the last dance. That would give him a chance to escort her home, maybe hold her hand while biking next to her, and, hope against hope, maybe get a kiss from her at her door.

All that dancing was hard work, and the hall got stuffy as the evening went on and the sweat started to flow, but everybody smelled the same, and nobody took notice.

The Other End of Town

When I was a small girl, my world was that corner of North-way, where my whole family lived. The baker and the shoemaker and the saddle-maker were our neighbors, and that was pretty much the size of it. My world didn't start to expand until I went to school or occasionally went on the train to Haderslev, eleven kilometers away.

The schoolhouse was a long yellow brick building just around the corner from us on Gammelvej. It was divided into two parts, with separate entrances. In one end lived the teacher for grades five to seven, Mr. Jepsen, with his wife, Anna, and their four children. There were just two classrooms, with grades one to four in one room and grades five to seven in the other. A young woman named Miss Petersen taught the first four grades. She was an extremely gentle, patient woman, and a marvelous storyteller. She whetted my appetite for learning about the larger world. (Our parents did not have the time to read to us kids; making a living was all they could handle.)

My incoming class consisted of my two boy cousins, William and Egon, and myself. In short order we were absorbed into the other classes. We learned our first math facts on a large abacus, and our letters were done on a slate board with a *griffel* (a slim, pointed stick of graphite, wrapped with colored paper around one end). Paper wasn't wasted in those days.

Schoolhouse.

Mr. Jepsen's classes were something else again. I could write volumes about his abstract teaching methods. A tall, lanky man, always dressed in a tweed suit, he had an ingenious mind and a hot temper. He was also a gifted musician, a talented playwright, and a songwriter. People came from the whole county when we held our school plays at the inn. We both feared and loved Mr. Jepsen. His classes were never dull.

I did my work, kept quiet, stayed out of trouble, and hoped that he would not notice me. My absolute worst nightmare came when he picked me to play the role of Cinderella in sixth grade. In the opening scene, I had to dance around the stage with a broom. As if that wasn't bad enough, I also had to sing a little song. Although Mr. Jepsen seemed well pleased with my performance, it cured me for life, and I have never been in a play since.

We lived close enough to the school that we could run home for noon dinner. Whoever was assigned to ring the hand bell after recess watched out for us and kept ringing it until they could see us galloping around the corner. That way we were never late for class.

I was enlarging my world. I shall continue my travels on Gammelvej. The church was on our left. Soon we came to the bend in the road with the big ugly station house on the right. It was built in the German style of yellow brick with red trim, and my father hated it. I have a vague recollection of going with my Grandmother Anne Sofie on the train to Haderslev. Every now and then the conductor came through the coupe and shoveled coal into the iron furnace to keep us warm. Unfortunately, the train was replaced with buses some years later, and the station house was turned into apartments. Living there was considered a terrible fate; those apartments were thought of as the slums of Fjelstrup.

So we passed the station and rounded another bend. We passed the barber shop, Niels Hagedorn's building business, and from there we came to Laurits Larsen's carpentry shop, another favorite spot of ours. It was a wonderful place, located in the end of a small house with a thick straw roof. It smelled of wood shavings and glue, and if we were lucky, Mr. Larsen would give us a lump of putty to play with. It was like dough and could be shaped into different things. I'll always remember how our hands smelled of linseed oil after playing with it.

Larsen's house and workshop.

In his shop, Mr. Larsen made windows and doors and cabinets for houses. But he had a sideline. All of the coffins for folks in town were made by him. In a shed in back of the house, a fancy black hearse was stored. When someone died, it was Mr. Larsen who took over the role of funeral director. He always had a couple of coffins stored in the loft above the shop. They were simple pine boxes, always painted white. At that time we did not have the little chapel next to the church, nor were people ever embalmed (and still aren't, as a matter of fact). People were buried within a couple of days of death and it never seemed to pose a problem.

Johanne and Laurits Larsen

Once notified, Mr. Larsen would bring the coffin to the house and help the women put the body into it and empty the room of furniture. They hung white sheets over the windows and stopped the clocks. All that was left on display were a couple of candles and a picture of Jesus.

Mr. Larsen had taken over the job from his father, and it continued to be handed down in the family. When our mother died in 1989, Mr. Larsen's grandson, Bent, provided the service.

Johanne and Laurits Larsen were best friends with my parents. They played cards together, and we often went on Sunday outings with them. When I grew up and traveled away from home, they kept track of me. Whenever I came back for a visit, we all cried big wet tears when it was time to say good-bye.

After Larsen's place and another slight bend in the road, we found ourselves back to the New-Way and South-way crossing—the other end of town! Those four corners were occupied by a gas station, an auto shop, the post office, and the house of the veterinarian, Dr. Arne From.

As I write about the people in my little town, and I think about many I haven't mentioned yet, I realize how important they were in my life. They lived their lives, raised their families, and worked their trades. As I grew up and left the village, many followed me in my travels. To this day, when I return, I am welcomed by those who are left. The older generation has, of course, found its place inside the wall, beneath the towers of the old church, and I always visit and remember them once again.

The Second Crossing

It took some years for me to grow big enough to travel on my own to the second of the two crossings that held our small village together. This was where the old road *(Gammelvej)*, Old-way, joins with the new straight thoroughfare called New-way *(Nyvej)*.

Mikael Møller's grain storage was the place where all the farmers brought their wheat, oats, and barley after harvest. I thought Mr. Møller must be very rich. He drove a fancy car, and neither he nor his wife associated with us or ever came to the inn. Their daughter was called

Gerda, like my sister, but she went to private school in Haderslev. She dressed in fancy clothes and never played with us.

The Møller storage was a busy, dusty place. About a dozen men worked for him, including my Uncle Herman. Without a doubt he was the town's largest employer. For his customers' convenience, he turned a small corner of his large red brick house into a tiny grocery store, run by Frederick Carstensen and his wife, Petra. There was so little space, Carstensen had to store a lot of his supplies in the loft. Years later I found out that the boys in town took advantage of the situation by asking for things they knew would send the poor man charging up those rickety stairs. While he was gone they would quickly stuff candy or licorice in their pockets. I was outraged when my brother told me this. From our earliest days, we had had it pounded into our heads by our parents that to steal even the smallest thing was a very serious matter. Of course, the thieving boys were the same ones who built an infamous tree house, and who fought their silly gang wars with neighboring town boys down in the meadow.

In that same cluster you would also have found Niels Hagedorn's building business and Christensen's tailor shop, where my brother, Willy, became an apprentice when he was fourteen. At Søren Thomsen's gas pump and auto shop, men gathered to smoke and spit and talk. The place was always in comfortable disarray.

The southwest corner was occupied by Hans Cornett's house, which also served as post office. He was the postmaster. His wife, Anna, operated the switchboard, pulling little plugs out and connecting them to the right parties. There were very few phones in town, so Anna had a lot of time on her hands, and she was the central news carrier for the region. Everyone knew that she listened in; sometimes she was even included in the conversation. If you wanted privacy, it was safer to get on your bike and go talk in your friends' kitchens.

Opposite the post office lived the veterinarian, Arne From. For years he was unmarried, and a lady named Anne Rasmussen served as his housekeeper. Dr. From was the son of a well-to-do farmer down the road. He was soft-spoken. We kids rarely saw him, let alone spoke to him. But we did know that he took care of sick animals, and eventually that led us to his house.

Gerda and I had a cat, much beloved and very spoiled. She was the most ordinary of farm cats, black and white, common in every way except for her fur. Despite all our caressing and brushing, I think you would say she had a bad hair day every day. Because of her disheveled appearance, we gave her the name Pjusk, a name that might be translated into English as "Tousled."

Pjusk developed a condition that caused her to sneeze and her nose to run. It was messy and bothersome, and we had to carry a rag to wipe her nose, a procedure all of us hated, especially Pjusk. One of us had the brilliant idea to take her to Dr. From. We put her in my bicycle basket and went to his house.

Anne Rasmussen appeared in response to the ringing doorbell. She was a stern and serious lady, rather intimidating to two rumpled kids like us. I was about nine. Since Gerda was older, she did the talking.

"Our cat is sick, and we would like the doctor to look at her," she told Anne. She told her the gory details about Pjusk's runny nose.

"You wait here," Anne said, and firmly closed the door on us. We stood waiting until she came back and brusquely told us to take the cat into the doctor's office.

We had never seen a doctor's office like this one. It had a big, fancy desk, big leather chairs, and many books. We could see that the good doctor did not treat goats or pigs in that fancy room! We were nervous, but all we could do was wait. Soon enough he appeared and we explained again about Pjusk's untidy problem. He seemed kind enough and smiled slightly, so we were reassured. After a while he took a look at our tousled cat. He went to a cabinet and brought out a small vial with some menthol crystals in it.

"See here," he said. "You take a few of these crystals and you put them in a small pot of water on the stove. When it begins to steam, you hold the cat over it for five to ten minutes. Do that for a week or two, several times a day, and you'll see, she will get much better."

We curtsied and said thank you as he ushered us out. As soon as we were home we set about giving Pjusk her first treatment. It turned out to be no easy task. The good-natured little cat we had known since her infancy turned to full fury. She fought the strong menthol vapor with all her might, but we held on, one of us holding her back legs, the other the

Fjelstrup volunteer fire department.

front. A pretty scene it was not, and the commotion brought our mother out to see what was going on. To say she was astounded to learn about our visit to the vet is an understatement, but she didn't yell at us about it.

Whether the treatments worked or Pjusk got better in self-defense I cannot say. I do know that we could not keep up with that furious display of cat power, and after a few days we gave up and went on to other things. Pjusk led a good long life, sometimes with and sometimes without her drippy nose.

More Neighbors

As I began to pay attention to people in the world beyond my immediate family, one of the men I noticed was the shoemaker across the way, Magnus Olsen. His daughter, Anna, was my age, and eventually she began to spend a lot of time at our house. Her mother, Johanne, had been married to a man who was killed in World War I, and Anna's half-brothers, Anders and Christian, were that first husband's sons.

Magnus was not the brightest man, but he was good and solid, and he could fix a pair of old boots or shoes better than anyone else. No matter

Minutes from first meeting of the fire department, in the handwriting of Solveig's father.

the shape of the shoes, Magnus would put new soles and heels on them, polish them, thread them with new laces, and send them out of his shop looking like new.

To me, though, that was not his greatest talent. Magnus was the town's bugle-blower. Out in his front hall hung a fancy silver bugle that we were never supposed to touch. It was used only when there was a fire in the area. There were few telephones then, so word would come quickly to Magnus, and he would go to the knoll by his house, his green cobbler's apron stretched over his round stomach as he drew in breath. He blew his bugle with long, clear tones that could be heard all over town. It was an impressive skill that gave him great dignity.

Within minutes, men from all the houses could be seen racing their bikes down around the corner to the firehouse. There was always a great deal of excited shouting as the old fire engine was pulled out. The men tossed their bikes any old place and swung themselves up on the benches as someone pulled the crank with all his might to get the engine started. Opposite the driver's side was a brass horn with a handle. That horn made long impressive sounds as the handle was pulled and pushed. Sixteen of the men in the neighborhood were members of the volunteer fire department that had been started by my father and Uncle Jokum in May of 1925.

Since there were only wells and water holes to draw water from, I don't really know if they ever saved a house, but they did try.

On the opposite corner of the crossroad was Andreas Nielsen's dry goods store. Andreas and his wife Dagmar did not mingle much with the rest of us, and we felt uncomfortable when we shopped at his store. I felt that it took all of his patience to wait for us to pick out a few glazed pictures for our scrapbooks, but since we seldom had any money, it wasn't a frequent problem.

Dagmar, on the other hand, fascinated us. She wore elegant clothes and when she took her dog—a Great Dane, the only one of its kind in the whole county—out for a walk, we hung out the windows to watch her. She tripped away, taking small mincing steps on her short legs, carrying her round little body very straight. She and the tall, spindly-legged dog, walking side by side, were quite a sight to see.

Dagmar's father, Mads, lived with them, tending their garden full time. I never heard if he had any other job.

On the fourth corner was a very stately white villa with a neat balcony and blue tiled roof. In it, Marie Bramsen, a widow and self-ordained queen mother of us all, lived with her maid. She got across to us clearly that she was much higher on the social ladder than we were. When we had to go to her house on an errand for our mother, we considered it an honor if we were invited in to sit on her embroidered chairs. She attended church regularly. The Bible was always next to her chair, and she never failed to show us the plant on her window sill that was named "Christ's Crown of Thorns."

In her cultivated little voice, she repeated the story of the thorny plant, regarding us piteously the whole time. The humble plant, she said, was the symbol of Jesus' sufferings for us. I got the idea that she thought we did not appreciate this, and did not take enough care of our appearance, possibly insulting Jesus as a result, but I knew that Jesus loved me because the picture over the altar in our church said, "Let the little children come to me."

I didn't think that Jesus minded my grimy face or my dingy apron.

After Mrs. Bramsen's husband died, she always dressed in black, as widows did. She even wore a black apron adorned with a bit of black lace at the top. She had a musty, slightly sweet lavender smell about her. I thought it was a ladylike smell, but now I realize that she had no access to either a bathtub or shower. Come to think of it, none of us did in that era, so in that sense, at least, we were all equal.

Child's Play

I have been often asked, "What did you do when you lived in that little village in Denmark? What was it like? How did you spend your time?"

In many ways we did the same things that children all over the world did then and do now. Some things were about playing, some were about learning, some were about taking part in our community in ways that changed subtly as we grew up.

We took gymnastics lessons in the winter, and I took piano lessons, requiring me to bicycle five miles to Christiansfeld where the teacher lived. (No vans, no carpools then!) Girls played ball against the wall in the school hallway during recess. In the spring we played games that would be familiar to anyone now, like hopscotch and jump rope, stickball and soccer. At that time of year, we made our own kites, too. Summer evenings, all the kids from the neighborhood gathered in the street and played ball games until it was dark and our mothers called us in. After school, we did a little babysitting—mostly traipsing up and down the street pushing a baby in a buggy for an hour or so. For that we might earn the grand total of twenty-five cents, but of course that did mean more then.

As soon as school ended for summer vacation, we began packing lunch and going to the beach seven miles away on our bicycles every day. Young people express surprise now to hear that there were no lifeguards and that we taught ourselves to swim in cold salt water. When I tell about the jellyfish, and how quickly we learned to avoid the ones with the red centers and long trailing stingers, kids now express great relief that they can swim in a pool.

Maybe it is even more surprising when I say that we did not have wristwatches. Instead, we drew a circle in the sand and planted a stick in the middle. From the shadow it cast, we knew when it was time to go home. On a good day we could get in three swims, but when our skin turned blue and our teeth began to chatter, we ran to roll up in our blankets until we were warm. We ate rye bread sandwiches and home-made fruit juice. So-called snack food was unheard of.

Although most of our fun came out of daily life (such as the activities in the barnyard) and whatever surprises it might offer, we of course had some toys. Every fall, when the men sawed up wood for the winter, our mother made dolls for Gerda and me. She took cloth from flour sacks, made arms and legs and a big body, and stuffed it all with fresh sawdust. On the face she embroidered eyes, nose, and mouth with brown yarn.

One year she made one we called Marie. After a year of hard use, she was old and grimy, and we got it in our heads to get rid of her. It was a dark, cold day when bursts of wind blew leaves down the path between the buildings, and raindrops crept down the windowpane. We sat at the window, leaning on our elbows, growing bored. This must explain our rash decision.

"Look at her," we grumbled, holding Marie up for inspection. "She is smelly and useless." We agreed we didn't need her anymore. Mother would make us a new one when the sawing was done. Besides, we each had a store-bought doll with real hair and blue eyes that opened and closed. Marie was ugly, and worse, she was homemade. So we decided to throw her into the wood stove. After all, she was made of sawdust!

We tossed her in on the flaming wood and watched through the grille as she burned away. We sat close together on the floor, looking at the flames. When we finally looked at one another both of us cried. We already missed Marie. Sure, she was ugly and dirty, and the sawdust in her arms and legs had packed down so that they were half empty, but she had still been soft and warm, and her mouth and eyes sewn with brown yarn had been smiling and friendly.

She was gone, and we missed her.

Boys were another matter entirely. Even in 1933 there were gangs, as there are here as I write this in 2001.

Boys from Fjelstrup met with boys from Sillerup down in the meadow by the creek, which was the dividing line between the two villages. They all came equipped with swords and spears made of wood. Holding their shields like Vikings, they fought ferocious territorial battles, accompanied by a lot of cursing and yelling.

I'm sure that a few black eyes and scrapes and bumps resulted from those melées, but no worse than any good mother could fix with the help of hot water, green soap, and strips of old sheets for bandages. I don't remember ever hearing of broken bones.

My brother, Willy, was of course a member of the Fjelstrup gang, along with all the neighbor boys. They built themselves a clubhouse in a tall oak tree some distance from our home. That's neither new nor old, either; grown men have always gathered. Now they call their clubs after animals with titles like the Moose, the Elks, the Lions, etc. One group couldn't think of a name and called themselves the Odd Fellows!

The boys' tree clubhouse was, of course, strictly off-limits to girls. It was an unwritten, clearly understood law. We knew that if we got caught up there, something terrible would happen to us, like a beating, dismemberment, or maybe baldness! Gerda and I were certainly not brave enough to take a chance with this kind of danger, so we eyed the place from an awed, curious distance.

Our cousin Lisse, on the other hand, was well known for her feisty behavior and the resulting scraped knees, torn clothes, and bruises. She drove her mother, our Aunt Hanne, to distraction with her antics, but she had the guts we lacked. It was she who thought up the master plan for getting back at those bullheaded boys. The perfect opportunity came when all the boys had to go to a soccer match out of town. Following Lisse's instructions, we found flat boards and wide sticks and set out to do our deed.

With the boards we scooped up freshly dropped cow pies and with the inch-wide sticks we managed to smear each step of the ladder leading up to the clubhouse. Lisse did the highest steps and we helped as we worked our way down, smearing each step with marvelous greenish-brown goop.

What sweet revenge! It was well worth the sick fear and nauseating smell. We knew the boys only went up in the house after dark, so they would feel the stuff before they saw it. Perfect.

For days afterwards we watched nervously, but nothing happened. The boys were hostile, nothing new, but they didn't suspect us. Soon we heard them sawing and hammering in the woodshed and we knew they were making new weapons. Of course they had put the blame on the Sillerup gang. Our clever mischief had set another war to brewing.

Today's gangs are a different concept. In the streets of Chicago, gangs fight on a daily basis, and the old wooden swords and spears of my brother's childhood play have been replaced with guns and knives. The fear of a beating has been replaced with fear of death.

Recently I heard a young Latino boy named Tony tell of his experiences with gangs and his flight from the city to our safer suburbs. As I thought about his story, I knew I had to record this aspect of our innocence. Gangs are not new, but they have become something very different from those in my childhood.

The Barnyard

I remember watching chickens and wondering why they couldn't fly. As Gerda said, they do have wings, just like other birds.

We had been watching chicks since they emerged from eggs, their little bodies still sticky from being inside the shell. Of course in less than an hour they dried up, got yellow and fluffy, and began stumbling around on their wobbly legs.

Within a week, the chicks learned to find water and food and to go into the sheltered cage our father had built. The cage could hold more than fifty little chicks. Along the sides were small windows, and we girls loved to look through them and watch the chicks. Once in a while a chick got sick and lay on the floor listlessly until our mother gently picked it up and took it into the kitchen. There she made warm soapy water and washed the dirt and dung off the yellow down. Next to the warm stove she made a nest of old rags and fed the sick chick with an eyedropper. Most of the time she was able to get it well enough to rejoin its siblings.

As the weeks went by, the chicks got feathers and flapped their little wings. On nice days they went out into the yard and scratched in the grass.

For us, this was play. We loved to watch them become chickens. But we did wonder why they never even tried to fly. We decided that their mother wasn't teaching them. Mother hens seemed to think about nothing but laying eggs.

"Maybe we could teach them," we said. "Then they could teach the others." What a plan it seemed! We could imagine the fun of watching chickens fly.

We got colored yarn from Mother's sewing basket and tied it around the legs of two chicks, green for Gerda, red for me.

In the corn loft, two windows faced the chicken yard. We took our little chicks up there to throw them down; surely they would fly then, because they would have to! When we tossed them out, they flapped their little wings frantically and squawked until they landed on the ground. Fortunately, the distance wasn't fatal. Meanwhile, we ran full speed down the stairs and recaptured them. Then it was back up to the loft, out the window again, for more flying lessons, on and on.

We thought: We'll do this every day for two weeks, right after school. And we did keep at it. The chicks began to recognize us and they scratched nervously when we entered the yard.

As the days went by, their wings seemed to grow stronger and we became ever more determined, but the chicks showed no interest in learning to fly. Two weeks of training went by, and still they crash-landed, protesting all the way. They flapped their wings unenthusiastically. Our dream of having the only flying chickens in Fjelstrup slowly faded.

Finally we told our mother about our failed efforts. We told her how hard we had tried and how we had wished so much to have prize chicks, and how disappointed we were.

She hugged us and smiled. "Chickens can't fly anymore," she said. "A long time ago, when they lived in the wild, they did. But now they have a barnyard life, and they just lay eggs for us."

She went on, drawing our attention elsewhere, to something exciting and instructive, because, as I have told you, in our little village playing and learning were often the same thing.

"I'm going out to check on the big brown Sussex hen who is sitting on our goose eggs. Why don't you come with me and see if they are picking holes in their shells yet. Geese are much easier to train, you know."

So it was that we gave up on those brainless chicks and turned our attention elsewhere.

It was peaceful and quiet in the barn where Mother had brought us. I carried a big bowl while she carried a kettle of warm water. She told us to speak softly so that I would not disturb the brown Sussex hen that was sitting on ten goose eggs.

One by one Mother took the eggs out from under the hen, and while holding them in the palm of her hand, she lowered them into the lukewarm water in the bowl. She whispered to me that if the egg felt buoyant and had some movement in it, we could count on there being a gosling inside. If the egg felt heavy and lifeless, it was a dud, and we would throw it away. She let me try to hold one of the eggs, with her hand under mine for safety's sake.

"Why do you have the big Sussex sitting on these eggs?" I whispered back. "Shouldn't a goose do it?"

She explained that we didn't have a mother goose left; they were all sold or cooked last winter. Besides, she said, geese tend to be flighty, whereas the Sussex was reliable and patient, with big soft wings. Goose eggs are quite large, but the hen was big enough to keep them nice and warm under her. Mother had bought the expensive eggs, so each gosling was important to us. After dipping all the eggs, we learned that only two were duds, and mother felt very lucky.

After a few more weeks, Gerda and Mother and I went out to check on the eggs again. Lo and behold, two of the little goslings were chipping holes in their shells. Within a few days all of the eggs were broken and the goslings were stumbling around in the straw by the mother hen. They seemed to recover much faster than baby chicks.

They were kept inside the barn for several weeks, eating huge bowls of gruel Mother made for them. Every day they grew bigger. Finally, on nice warm days, she let them out in the new grass. They frolicked around, but when Mother Sussex detected any sign of danger, she clucked and spread her wings, and the yellow goslings ran for cover.

Of course Mother Nature had not intended a chicken to be the mother of eight small geese. As the gruel went into the gosling stomachs, they grew too big for the hen's big brown wings. When they tried to fit themselves under her, the poor hen started to levitate. Her feet could barely reach the ground as those frisky babies battled for cover.

The real nervous breakdowns came when spring rains began.

At the first sign of a sprinkle, Mother Sussex started clucking and spreading her wings so the babies could come in out of the rain. But the goslings liked water; it was in their nature to splash in puddles and poke in the mud. In her despair, their poor stand-in mother ran in circles trying to gather her unruly brood together, to no avail.

Mother watched this from the kitchen window and finally decided she had to relieve the hen of her responsibilities. A safe pen lined with straw was constructed for the goslings, and Mother Sussex was taken back to the chicken yard.

Now it was our turn. Gerda and I took over the parenting role. We picked our favorite goslings, marking them with colored yarn around their legs as we had with the chicks. Gerda called hers Skat and I called mine Palle. Alas, they were too young for flying lessons. So we gathered our aprons up in front to form a pocket, and we carried our goslings everywhere we went. We sat in the grass and talked to them while we stroked their feathers and crooned their names again and again. Within a couple of weeks all we had to do was open the door and call them, and they came running, willingly hopping into our aprons while the rest of the flock followed along as we walked into the field.

Of course we soon found out that Mother Nature was stronger than our Mother Love. We were given the job of leading the flock to a water hole about two hundred yards from the barn. Skittish as they are, the ganders picked up any little sound or movements, and we just knew that when they started scrapping and yapping, the whole flock, without fail, would make a turnabout and streak back to the barn. Believe me, those geese did not need flying lessons. As much as Gerda and I tried to soothe and distract them, once they got excited, there was no stopping them. Long necks outstretched, they half-flew, half-ran close to the ground, covering the distance much faster than we could run.

Sometimes it took two or three tries to get the whole flock to water, but once they saw where they were, they were ecstatic. They hopped right in and floated around gracefully. A big willow tree hung over the end of the pond, and they swam around under the branches, catching bugs and nibbling on leaves.

All was well in goose land until we heard our mother calling us home. Getting them out of the water was a new problem, but we had our reward for all the cuddling and love we had bestowed on Skat and Palle. When we called them, they stopped paddling and came to us. Then when we began our walk back home, the rest of the flock followed along.

The barn, of course, was never still. Pigs grunted and squealed. Cows shook their heads and swished their tails to get rid of pesky flies. They were noisy, too, as they chewed their food over and over. My father told me they had two stomachs and chewed their food twice. I watched them swallow and then bring up more food from the first stomach and start in again. All of this was very interesting to me. I spent many hours watching and listening to animals.

One day I was in the storage area looking for chicken eggs, which were sometimes laid in hidden places, when I found a beautiful, intricate spider web. Below it was a pile of dead flies and bugs. I sat for quite a while, waiting for the spider so that I could see him at work, but my patience ran out. I got an old dirty glass jar and took it into the cow-barn.

I caught a fly without a thought; there were millions of them bothering the cows and pigs. With my hand over the jar to keep the fly from escaping, I went back to the web. There I carefully caught hold of the fly's wings and slowly dropped him into the web, where he was immediately stuck in the silky strings, despite much buzzing and struggling.

Soon the spider appeared, a handsome fellow, gray with long legs. He waited until the fly wore out and got still. Then he gripped the fly with his long legs and paralyzed him. He sucked the juice from the fly and let him drop onto the pile of other dead flies.

It was fascinating, and I knew it was just the spider's job. He had a purpose, like all living things. I watched for quite a while as the spider returned and deftly repaired his net where the struggling fly had torn it. When I left, the web was as perfect and beautiful as before, and the spider had retreated to his hiding place to wait patiently for his next doomed guest.

Good Times

A sure sign of fall was that the apples on the tall old tree in the garden were ripe for picking. This was an all-family project and an important day we anticipated with pleasure. We hauled our ladders, buckets, and baskets, and Father assigned each of us those jobs that suited us. Brother Willy was chosen to climb the highest branches, because he was quick and sure-footed. Gerda and I had the job of picking from the lower limbs or whatever we could reach from chairs and stools. Mother and Maggie, the maid, gathered the apples and took them to storage in the loft.

Father reminded us not to bruise or drop the precious fruit, as any mark could make it rot. The apples had to last us all winter. You couldn't buy fruit very often in country stores, so we ate the things Mother had canned, and also some hard pears we called winter pears. The big red apples were important, and picking them was wonderful fun.

✳

Father was mumbling. He was using an apple picker, a cloth bag fastened to a long pole. Around the edge of the bag there was a metal rim with a saw-toothed edge. When it tore the apple from the branch it fell into the bag.

He was still muttering as he came down the tree with his basket full. He showed us some of the apples, each with a small hole with tooth marks around the edge.

"What can this be?" he asked. "I wonder if some small animal has come into our garden to taste our apples."

We gathered around to assess the damage. Only Gerda hung back, shuffling her feet and acting bored.

Father noticed and called to her. "Little Gerda," he said, "do you know where these holes came from?" She came over and he put his arm around her and looked in her face.

She sniffled. "Oh, Dad, do you remember when you told us not to pick any apples before they were ripe, because we would have to throw them away if they were sour?"

Father nodded, yes he remembered. So Gerda went on to tell how she had climbed the tree. When she saw a nice red apple, she took a careful little bite out of it. If it was still sour, she let it hang and went on to try another one.

"I didn't pick them and throw them away," she said. Tears were coming now. "I left them to ripen like you said."

He smiled and held her closer. "I'm glad you did as I told you, Gerda," he said gently, "but next year you must be a little more patient and wait a little longer before you taste them."

That evening Mom made a Danish apple cake with whipped cream from those "tooth apples."

Making the best of what we had available was just the way life was, and my mother's skills at cooking and sewing were important. And of course we were fortunate because much of our food was right where we lived, with farmland that belonged to the inn and the animals in the barnyard.

The family's skills became even more crucial during the severe economic depression of the thirties. I was still a little girl, so I wasn't worried about the state of the world, but I do remember hearing my mother and Grandmother Anne Sofie talk about how to use an old coat or dress to make a new one. They spent hours ripping seams open and washing and pressing pieces, then cut and sewed a brand-new garment for one of us children. Often this was out of something that had been hanging in the closet for years.

Once I received a new dress made from two dresses outgrown by Gerda. The top was solid blue and the skirt was tan and blue plaid that matched the top quite well. Grandma made a bow out of the plaid material and fastened it at the neckline. I wore it to a school social where I had to recite a poem. I was so nervous, I recited the same stanza twice, even though I had had it memorized for weeks. The pretty dress looked nice, but it did not give me more confidence.

There was a shortage of butter, and we began to make it in our own kitchen. To me, this was exciting. Mother somehow got cream from somewhere, and she added a bit of acid, explaining that it helped turn it into good butter. She placed a large metal jug on two chairs in the kitchen. The jug had a wooden lid and a plunger on top. We took turns pumping the wooden plunger slowly and evenly, up and down. I was too small to reach the plunger, so they gave me a wooden stool to stand on. It was exciting to see the cream form into ever larger lumps until the plunger could no longer be pushed through it. Mother then scraped the butter into a big basin. I can remember standing on my stool, watching her knead and slap the pale butter with a flat wooden spoon until all the liquid was worked out of it. The leftover liquid was buttermilk. It tasted wonderful with a spoonful of sugar added.

While these necessary but intriguing activities were going on, I didn't notice that business at the inn had fallen off. Everyone was having to be careful with money and so coming to the inn, and spending money there, was not a priority for families, and of course our family's income was reduced.

At Christmas, we prepared in the usual ways. Early in the month we went out as a family to gather evergreen branches for the Advent wreath Mother would make in the kitchen. She decorated it with red ribbons and four candles and it was hung from the ceiling in our living room. Each Sunday, a candle was lit and we sang the Advent song.

One Sunday, several weeks before Christmas, our father sat Willy and Gerda and me down and talked to us seriously.

"There will not be any Christmas presents this year," he told us, "because we are having a very bad year and money is short. So," he went on, "the rubber boots you need will be your only presents."

I don't remember feeling sad at this news, except that he looked so unhappy himself. I thought it was good that he told us how things were without embellishing. I didn't really care about presents. Christmas was such a happy time, with dancing and singing around the tree, and those were the things that mattered, the things I loved best.

On Christmas Eve after church we had our usual wonderful dinner. Mother had cooked one of the geese she had raised. As always, we first ate rice porridge that had one almond hidden in it. The person who found the almond got a prize, a little pig made from marzipan. Later, Father told us that he got the almond in his very first spoonful, but he kept it hidden in his cheek until we were all done, not to ruin the suspense.

Our custom was to go out to the barn before dinner with a bowl of porridge for the little elves (*nisser*). After we finished our meal, we ran out to the barn to see if the elves had been there. It was exciting to see the empty bowl and imagine hungry little elves eating the porridge. We could practically smell them, and we wondered if they were hidden somewhere in the straw and hay. I didn't find out until years later that Maggie went out to the barn and scraped the porridge into another container while we were eating our dinner.

While the dishes were being done, Father lit the candles on the tree. We weren't allowed to come into the room until they were all lit. That particular year, the tree was smaller and it was placed in the fancy parlor where we had eaten dinner. Later I was told that it was done that way to save the fuel it would have taken to heat up another room.

I thought it was the most beautiful tree ever. The candles lit up the place, and we held hands and sang Danish Christmas songs as we walked around the tree. We were all so happy in that room that I think even my parents forgot to worry for a little while.

Sure enough, we got rubber boots and put them on right away, but Mother had also made dresses for Gerda's and my dolls, and Dad had made a bow and some arrows from sticks in the hedgerows for Willy.

There was more to come, to our surprise. Maggie was whispering and nudging Knud, our young farmhand, to do something. "Come on, Knud," she urged, "bring them in."

Knud muttered something and his face got red, but she kept at him. "Sure they're good enough," she said. "Sure they'll like them."

Finally, Knud relented. He went out to the barn and returned with two doll beds! He looked embarrassed as he tried to explain that he had made them from margarine boxes from Uncle Jokum's storeroom out back.

"I wanted to p-paint them a pretty color, but all I c-could find was b-brown barn paint, and then the b-brushes were stiff," he stammered.

Gerda and I hardly heard his apologies, we were so overjoyed with those doll beds. We hugged Knud and then hugged him again until tears came to his eyes.

All our Christmases were full of joy, but that Christmas, and those presents, were especially wonderful. Simple brown doll beds made by a young shy farm boy helped to make for us the very best of times.

Grandmother Anne Sofie's Visits

One of the big events in my life was a visit from Grandmother Anne Sofie. After Grandfather Carl Sofus's untimely death, she made her home with her oldest son, Jørgen Ahrenkiel, whose farm was on the other side of Haderslev in a town called Fredsted. Grandmother made her way to us on the train and later on the bus with her old battered suitcase. It must have been a cumbersome trip for her, but two or three times a year we greeted her arrival with great happiness and much affection. She usually stayed for a couple of weeks.

She was a tall, stately lady, always dressed in black in the custom for widow ladies, but this did not make her seem stern, as she was sweet and kind and soft-spoken. She was gifted, too; her hands were never idle. Besides the sewing she did with my mother, she knitted new caps and mittens and stockings for us, and as we grew taller she crocheted rows to the bottoms of the dark red woolen under-slips that we wore every day. She made aprons for us to wear over our dresses to school, and she mended and repaired clothes for the whole family.

Best of all, though, was when she told us stories. While she knitted or crocheted, we sat on the floor and listened to her telling stories—wonderful, happy stories about princesses and kings, about castles and white horses, beautiful gowns and fancy balls. She spoke so softly, we had to be quiet to hear her, but as she wove those tales on and on, we never tired of listening.

Now that I have learned a lot from life, I sometimes wonder: Did she tell those stories to us so that she herself could, for a little while, escape the harshness of her own life, the brutal husband, the many children, the small ones who died, the sons lost in war? She seemed happy and peaceful when she spoke to us.

All of Anne Sofie's stories had happy endings.

True Community

My childhood was spent in a small town, a place of great simplicity compared to the rushed, busy, plugged-in world of today.

The most important thing I learned there was that we belonged to a community of people who cared, people who watched our behavior and called us to task if we behaved unacceptably. We learned tolerance and forgiveness as we observed people who did not think alike managing nevertheless to get along. One might wonder that I remember so many people's names and qualities, right down to what they wore and how they walked, but remember that we spent all of our time among one another in a way that was real, that wasn't what today we call "virtual reality." Although we heard the radio, programming was unsophisticated, and movies were not like what we see now. I had time and a lot of interaction with others, young and old, so I really got to know my neighbors in a way you don't when you just wave as you back out of your driveway in your car.

Fjelstrup had our share of what one might call "originals," and I want to describe a few of them, emphasizing the patience and accommodation that people allowed them. In Fjelstrup, even though there weren't so many inhabitants, there was still a range of character and circumstance. Some people were rich and some were poor. Some were good and others not so good. We kids grew up seeing love, jealousy, strength, and weakness, as kids now see, if they are looking. But what was different, I think, for me, was the undercurrent of unity, caring, and accountability that was present and possible in such a close-knit community. To this day, after more than fifty years away, I still feel at home when I return for a visit. I hope as much for my grandchildren when they recall their own growing up and their own hometowns someday, telling stories to grandchildren of their own.

But now let me tell you about some our "characters," and about some more of the things that occupied us as children.

Take Peter Smithy. That wasn't his real name, but he worked in Carl Hollesen's blacksmith shop. His peculiarity was that he never bought any new clothes. He wore whatever people gave him, whether the clothes fit him or not, and once the clothes were his, they were never again washed. He also had an odd diet. His daily fix was two strong beers and two shots of akvavit schnapps—first thing in the morning. I saw him take his walk to the grocery store every day with his oversized rubber boots sloshing around his skinny legs. He was odd, but he was also a good worker and an excellent horseshoer, so people accepted him and his habits.

Then there was Grete. She must have been young once upon a time, but as long as I knew her she was called Old Grete. I believe she lived with her mother until the old woman died and left Grete homeless. Our teacher, Mr. Jepsen, fixed up a very modest apartment for her upstairs in the barn next to the schoolhouse. She made her living working at odd jobs in different houses as she was called on. She helped us at the inn with dishes after big parties. When we kids climbed the ladder to bring her bunches of wildflowers, she was always pleased and happy. Mr. Jepsen also got her into the town choir, and many a time I heard my mother despair over Grete's inability to carry a tune. No one had the heart to tell her how awful she sounded, though, because she was proud to be a part of the choir.

Jørgen Grøndahl lived with his old mother down the road not far from us, surrounded by the biggest junk heap I have ever seen. We did not dare go near his place, but we were curious. He had a small homemade wagon and an old horse. One of the wheels was smaller than the other so that it leaned to one side, but that didn't bother him. He was a wheeler-dealer and managed to make a living with it.

I remember others, like "White Mads with the red eye," who, I learned later, was an albino. After a long bachelorhood he married a woman named Margrete whose fear of dentists eventually left her completely toothless. Mads didn't seem to mind her looks, and they had a good marriage and some nice children. The townfolks shared their happiness. No one thought that eccentricity or odd looks should be a reason for disliking or ignoring someone.

Mr. Zielke's story is a little different. His house was right where the road turned, in plain view from our windows. He was a saddlemaker, a good one, I was told, and he also fixed harnesses and straps for farmers and others who owned horses and wagons. His shop, situated in the front part of his house, smelled nicely of leather and saddle oil mixed with pipe tobacco. He was a short, red-haired man with a surly temper.

He had a second job as well, serving as cashier for the local State Health Insurance. He took pride in the assignment. It worked like this. When anyone needed to visit a doctor, someone from the family had to visit Mr.

Zielke first and get a "sick slip" *(syge seddel)*, a simple transaction. On the rare occasion that I was the one to go, I dreaded it, as I found him snoopy and intimidating, and he made me squirm with embarrassment.

He would glare at me and grumble, hardly visible through the heavy cloud of smoke from his pipe, which he never seemed to take out of his mouth. "So!" he would say. "Someone sick again, huh! What is it this time?"

I wasn't even eight years old, and very shy, so all I could do was stand there under his barrage, shuffling my feet and hanging my head low, wishing for the paper slip so I could get away. He always took his time, puffing away and carrying on about how people ran to the doctor for every simple thing, taking advantage of the system and the taxpayers. (And where do you hear that now?!)

Finally he taunted me, "What's the matter with you? Can't you hold your head up straight? Maybe you have water in your ears?" As his torment cascaded over me, my face turned redder than a beet. Finally he got up from his stool, toddled over to his big safe, and hid the dial as he turned it—in case I might come back in the night and rob him, I suppose!

As cashier, Mr. Zielke had a lot of dealings with Dr. Westergård. The good doctor lived a short way down, on North-way, in an stately villa. He was the doctor not only for our small village, but for all the farms and small communities for miles around. He was an elegant man about whom little was known except that he had once been in a mental hospital. He was kind and gentle, and seemed to be a good enough doctor, but, as you might guess, Mr. Zielke was the curse of his life.

The doctor, a sensitive man, was the prime target of the saddlemaker's taunts. Even though I was only a child, I understood perfectly when the doctor finally flipped. One day his anger built into a terrible rage, and he appeared at Zielke's house in the early morning, bent on killing his tormentor.

Mr. Zielke's wife and many children lived in other parts of the house; it was his wife, Lene, who made us aware of this huge calamity. When the doctor appeared, obviously enraged, she burst out the door and ran up the road, stirring up dust with her morning slippers, all the while wringing her hands in her apron. She screamed for my father, who had, over the years, become a village peacemaker in times of trouble, a kind of "fixer" for despair.

"Hans! Hans!" she cried. "Come quick, the doctor is going to kill my husband!"

My mother immediately sent us children upstairs into the bedroom. She told us to stay still, and she went out, locking the door behind her. We didn't mind, because we had a clear view of the excitement from the window. I remember thinking that it wouldn't be such a loss to be rid of Mr. Zielke, but I felt sorry for poor Lene, since he was, after all, her husband, and the father of their many children.

We saw Father running to the house. Shortly after he went inside, he came out holding Dr. Westergård by the hand. He sat with him until the ambulance came and took him away. To my knowledge, no one in the area ever heard from the doctor again, while Mr. Zielke went right on, being himself.

※

One of the ways we honored our community was by paying attention to the sick and to the deceased.

For example, there was poor Chresten, a nice boy, not too dumb, not too smart. Before he got sick, he was nothing special. Then everyone in his family became special, even his little sister Marie Cecelie and his tiny mother, whom we hardly knew.

They lived in a small house up in the field away from most of the village houses. We began to hear our mothers talking quietly about them, their voices dark with concern.

"Have you heard about poor little Chresten?" one said. Another answered, "We saw the doctor driving by this morning." The mothers tried not to talk when we were around, but rumors flew.

One morning, at precisely ten o'clock, the church bells rang. We all knew what that meant. Someone had died, and it had to have been Chresten.

Our teacher told us after the morning hymn. With tears in her eyes, her face flushed and sad, she said, "Little Chresten is no longer with us. He died last night of pneumonia."

Of course we were sad, and sorry we had paid him so little attention when he was alive, when he was nothing special. As it was, though, we had another

chance. Because he had been in our second grade class, we would go to the funeral.

First we went to his home, where he lay in his white coffin in the parlor. After the pastor spoke and we sang, and after his parents said their good-byes, we went up to the coffin and touched Chresten's small, cold hands.

Dead, he was a kind of hero. He had fought and lost, but now he had an elevated status.

After we had touched him, we all said another prayer and then they put the lid over him and carried him to the black hearse. The hearse was quite elegant, with black crepe around it. Two of the town's best horses were ready to pull it to the churchyard.

Each of us classmates carried a basket with greenery and flowers, and we were carefully instructed to walk in front of the hearse and drop the flowers and greens along the way. "Not too fast," we were told. "Make them last all the way to church."

Here was something we could do for Chresten, a way we could make it up to him that we had shown him such little regard.

As the horses began to move and we began our slow, proud procession, the church bells rang. We spread the contents of our baskets onto the ground, careful to distribute them as we had been told, right up to the church gates.

This was a powerful experience. Though we were small children, we were included in the services, in the honor paid to this little boy, and in this way we could show that we cared. Little Chresten mattered to the village, and so did we.

The coffin was placed in the church nave. We second-graders sat close together on a bench below. The organ played, people sang and prayed, and then Chresten was carried to the hole that had been dug for him in the churchyard.

For months and years I passed by his little white stone. When I am home even now, I make sure to visit his grave. I said good-bye to him a long time ago. Some people die forever, but not Chresten. I think of him, and in this way, he is alive still. So it is with memory.

Another time, we had to honor an old man who had died, and we were gloomy at the prospect. "Why us?" my sister, Gerda, asked. "Willy is older and yet he never has to go."

Mother had made a wreath for old Ivar, who had died the day before. He and his wife Lene had lived down the road a bit, just the two of them, with no children. It was only right that we pay respects, Mother said, giving us our orders several times until they were ingrained in our brains.

So we trudged off with our clean hands, combed hair, and of course, the wreath.

Lene and Ivar's house was quite small and low, with a thick straw roof. It was next to the creek, and the dampness made moss grow on the straw. We went past the pump, up to the back door. (The front door was seldom used, and never by children.)

We knocked, but nobody came, so we knocked harder, with our knuckles. Certainly we could not leave a wreath by the door and go away.

Finally we heard Lene's shuffle from inside. When she opened the door, Gerda, the older of us two, spoke. "Hello, Mrs. Ivarsen," she said. Both of us curtsied. "Our mother sends you her greetings, and this wreath." She handed it to Lene.

"Thank you," Lene said, rather matter-of-factly. "Come on in."

Now came the worst part, the part we dreaded so much but knew we had to do because it was part of the ritual.

"Come and see Ivar," Lene said as she shuffled ahead, carrying our wreath. Oh, we hated this! We had known Ivar our whole lives—we didn't need to see him dead! But we followed along as we had been told to do.

As was customary, the parlor had been stripped of furniture and of pictures. Sheets had been hung over the windows and against the wall by Ivar's coffin. A picture of Jesus hung above him, and there were candlesticks on each side of the coffin.

We peered into the coffin at Ivar. Even his fingernails were clean! We had certainly never seen him in a white shirt.

Lene began to talk mournfully. She was standing at the head of the coffin. "Wouldn't you know he would leave me here to take care of everything?"

she said. "How am I supposed to get the milk jug up the hill in the morning and take care of the chickens and the pig?" On and on she complained.

They only had one pig!

She worked herself up more and more, and to emphasize her dismay, she slapped Ivar on his clean bald head once and once again and then again, little slaps of frustration.

Ivar didn't mind, of course, but we did as we waited for her tirade to end.

Finally she said—to Ivar, not to us—"You just lie there while I do all the work!" Then she led us out of the room. She gave us cookies and fruit juice and asked us, "What are your names?" She spoke gruffly, but we knew she was still angry with Ivar.

"Gerda and Solveig," we said, "from over at the inn."

"Oh yes, Martha Petersen's girls."

We nodded our heads, and ate our cookies, one of each kind, and drank our juice at her kitchen table with its flowered oilcloth covering. As soon as we could do so politely, we got up to leave.

We shook Lene's hand and curtsied again, and then, Hallelujah, we got out of there, lickety-split!

Trauma Days

I do not mean to make light of anyone's suffering. All of us have days in our past that were so traumatic we remember the details forever. We remember where we were and what we were doing. For me, it was that kind of day when my mother was attacked by a steer. She had been moving the cattle in the field when it happened, and she went into shock or some kind of breakdown.

Gerda and I were playing in the attic with old bottles and interesting junk from the boxes up there. We were about seven and nine years old, used to entertaining ourselves in those days before television.

The attic was directly above a guest room used by visitors who stayed overnight at the inn. We slowly became aware of a haunting, hollow, moaning sound, like that of a wounded animal. We listened, wondering what it might be and where it was coming from.

After a while we became concerned enough to go downstairs to the kitchen. When we asked our maid Maggie about the sound, she wouldn't look at us. We saw tears on her face. Grandmother Elise was there, too, and she took us into the empty pub-room. She told us to sit over at a corner table, as far as we could get from the sound, and she talked to us very quietly.

"Your mother has been hurt," she said. "A cow went after her when she was leading it to another grazing spot. The cow pushed her down and stabbed at her with its horns." She went on to tell us that Mother had been rescued by a farmer, Peter Ravn, who carried her home.

Gerda and I were dumfounded, too scared to speak or even cry. Grandmother Elise went on, "Your Uncle Jokum drove into Haderslev to get your father. They'll be here with the doctor very soon." We knew that our father had gone to Haderslev, eleven kilometers away, to attend a funeral. By now we were both sobbing, but Grandmother told us that our mother would be all right, and we should just sit there and be still and wait. Then she left us.

Though it was growing dark in the room, no one had thought to turn on the lights. Gerda and I huddled together, listening to that awful sound. After a while Maggie came and took us into the kitchen. We heard a car come, and we saw our father run through the kitchen into the room where they had taken our mother. What went on in there we never learned, but the eerie moaning soon stopped. The doctor came and went, and Maggie fed us some supper and took us upstairs to bed. She was crying again as she hugged us, but she told us we would see Mother tomorrow.

Mother recovered, though she was very quiet and weak for a long time. She was sweet, she hugged us, but she was different.

Some weeks later it was arranged that she should go to Roskilde to stay with some friends. The town of Roskilde is near Copenhagen, all the way across the country. Willy and Gerda were sent along with her so that she would not get lonely and homesick, but they said I was too little, and I had to stay home. I so badly wanted Mother to get better and return to her sweet self, I didn't make any fuss about being left behind. I would be with my father, and my bed was moved next to his, and as always, I followed him around wherever he went.

I do not remember how long Mother was gone, but one day, very early in the morning, Maggie came into the bedroom. "Solveig," she said. "It is time to get up. This is the day you are going with your father to get your mother." She had packed a big basket with food and drinks, and my best dress was laid out, my shoes were polished, and I was to wear my red velvet jacket.

My father was getting the car ready; I now know it was a black Model T Ford. There were flower vases on the panel between the doors, and Maggie had put flowers in them. As we drove, my father spoke to me, pointing out things along the way, but I was too excited to speak.

We picked them up at the ferry site where the boat came in from the island of Fyen. I didn't see my brother and sister, though they were both there; I only saw Mother, and I cried. She was so beautiful, dressed in a light coat and cloche-style hat, and she looked well. I didn't want to speak. All I wanted was to be near her, and I wanted her to be well.

Our lives went on and she got stronger. She smiled again, and once in a while she even sang as she used to. Still, there were signs that all was not well. Her neck was stiff and she had trouble braiding and pinning up her long brown hair. There was talk about cutting it short, as the fashion for that was starting. She worried about it, but after much talk in the kitchen, she must have been convinced, and one day she and my father drove in to Haderslev. When they returned she had short hair. It didn't matter. Her smile and her love had not changed.

Now I realize it was about that time my father began to think about leaving the inn.

Last Days

Hans and Martha—Mother and Father—lived on. They retired and moved to a smaller house nearby, on South-way. Their three children had gone into the world they had read so much about. They returned for visits, and Father listened to them tell about their adventures. It was hard not to brag. When they returned with grandchildren, Hans took the children all over town.

Hans had plaques on the wall honoring him for his many accomplishments. In his drawer he kept a medal given to him by the Danish king for his good work for his town and country.

In time they sold a piece of land, bought tickets, and went to visit their wandering children. They quietly observed their new lifestyles and listened to them talk in languages they did not understand.

The years passed, and one day the inevitable phone call came. Hans had been taken to the hospital on a Sunday after church. It was all so fitting. He stayed alive until the children arrived to say good-bye. Then he closed his eyes and went away gently, with great style and dignity. He was eighty-six years old. When the church bells called for his last service, the church filled with people whose lives he had touched. He was buried in the family plot beside his parents and family members, just south of the church door.

Martha, in her widow years, seemed to stay in touch with him. When she died at the age of ninety-two, she too departed with dignity and grace. It was an early spring day, and she held yellow daffodils in her gentle hands. She was surrounded by her loving family, but the last person she spoke to was Hans. The bond between them was never broken.

Father: Hans Petersen
Born 1893; Died 1977

January 31, 1977. It was a winter day, not so very cold. My brother, Willy, and I had flown back to Denmark, and our cousin Lisse had picked us up at the small airport in Skrydstup. We were tired, not only from the long flight, but also from waiting in Copenhagen for six hours for the shuttle flight to South Jutland.

Cousin Lisse greeted us in her quiet way at the airport, and then when we were in the car, suitcases tucked away in the trunk, and on our way, she spoke. She said, "Your father is still living. There is still life in him." We did not say much in reply. We drove toward the hospital in the town of Haderslev. An elevator took us up a couple of floors, and down the long hall we saw a small person sitting on a chair outside one of the doors.

It was our mother. As we came closer, she looked up and saw us. Her eyes were tired and her face very pale. We folded into her arms, giving and getting comfort. We didn't cry. We were together, holding and hugging.

"They're nursing Dad," she said, "but you can see him soon." She seemed sad but resigned. We waited until the nurse came to us and said we could go in.

There is a quiet that takes over at times like these. A different kind of stillness, as though God is present in the room. It was that way when my first husband, Ray, died. This is a time that belongs to Him, and we are just bystanders.

Mother stood by Father's bed. "The children have come home," she said, sobbing.

I went to him and bent close. His eyes were shut, there were tubes in his nose, and he couldn't speak.

"Dad," I said, "we are here, Willy and I, we just got off the plane." I straightened out his fingers and stroked his shoulders. He moved his hand to my face and touched my cheek. His eye teared. He had heard me.

I kept on talking softly to him, squeezing that hand that had held mine a thousand times, held it inside his deep pocket on cold winter nights. His hands, so capable, that had fixed things and made them better.

After we were home I realized that Willy had not spoken to Dad. He hadn't seemed able to move from the end of the bed. His face had been flushed and he made no move to go to our father. I didn't urge him.

When we were alone I asked him why.

"I couldn't," he said. "I just couldn't talk." He could see that I was puzzled. He went on. "I didn't want to cry in front of my father," he said. "Dad never cried. I never saw him cry."

He turned away, tears in his eyes.

Mother: Martha Cathrine Ahrenkiel Petersen
Born 1896; Died 1989

My mother, Martha, was the third child of twelve born to Anne Sofie and Carl Sofus Ahrenkiel. She was the second child to be called Martha. The first Martha died in infancy. Three brothers, Jørgen, Carl, and Sofus,

The Ahrenkiel family with five of their twelve children and Grandpa Thomsen.

preceded her. She became her father's favorite. After her, three more girls were born: Ella, Didde (Kirstine), and Alma. Last came Johannes and Thomas. Three other babies were born and died soon after.

To others, her family life looked prosperous and well-ordered, but a closer look would have shown that it was far from that. In this day and age we might call it dysfunctional. Her father, Carl Sofus, owned a good-sized farm and he excelled in the dairy business. He won acclaim and medals for his excellent products such as cheese and butter. One of those medals, a large ornate silver piece, was given to me. My grandmother Sofie had it made into a pin and can be seen wearing it in some of her pictures. I have memories of Grandmother Sofie, but only photographs and stories about my grandfather, who died long before I was born.

He was a tall, handsome man, and I believe that his selfishness, pride, and brutishness show in his photographs. He wooed Anne Sofie, one of two daughters of a well-to-do farmer. She too was tall and slim, an attractive girl who was charmed by Carl Sofus. At first she would not have known that he had a frightening mean streak that surfaced when he drank alcohol.

Mother told me that he would come home from his weekly trips into the town of Haderslev drunk. His children dreaded the sound of his horse and wagon, for his moods frightened them as he shouted orders and brutalized their mother. If she denied him, he flew into rages. In self-defense she would run to the barn and bury herself in stacks of straw and hay. In his fury, he stabbed with a pitchfork, searching for her.

Mother told me how she talked gently and quietly to him, calming him down so that she could lead him back into the house, where he fell asleep in a stupor. Later she would go to the barn and bring her mother back.

This fear of alcohol stayed with my mother all her life. I believe that she and Father had an understanding about it, because in all the years we lived at the inn, I never saw him take a drink with the guests.

Grandfather Carl Sofus's life came to a predictable but no less sad end. Returning from another of his Haderslev trips, drunk and angry as usual, he took his gall out on his horse as he took off the harness. The horse kicked him in the stomach. He was carried into the house in great pain. An infection set in, and he died soon after.

I have listened to my mother and watched her face as she told the story several times about her two younger brothers being sent into the parlor to say their farewells to this man, their father whom they had feared and hated all their lives. They were only small boys, but as they came to the coffin, they kicked it with their boots and said, "Good! We're glad you are dead."

Even as an old woman, my mother cried, recalling this incident.

As was customary, Martha was sent to work in a good home at the age of fourteen, soon after her confirmation. In this way, a young girl was trained for her future life as a housekeeper, wife, and mother. Martha was a pretty girl with a perfect oval face and blue eyes. She had thick brown hair and in all the pictures I have of her, I see the same gentle smile that became so familiar and beloved to me. She told me she did have other suitors, but once Hans Petersen saw her, he wasn't about to let anyone else near her. They danced all the dances the night they met and he walked her home. She was impressed with his courtesy and his good manners, and from that day on they were totally committed to one another.

My parents' love was an affair that lasted a lifetime. Because of war and strife in Europe, it would be years before they could marry and start their life together at the inn in Fjelstrup, but they knew they were meant to be together, and of course they were. Their struggle to marry is in many ways a story of Denmark at that time, for they followed the old ways in setting out on their lives, and their love affair, delayed for so long, was a part of the struggle with Germany.

The Germans figured in my youth, too, of course, in World War II, and in the second part of my story, I will tell about their occupation of our village.

For now, though, I am remembering my parents. Their love story is so precious to me, I will close this section by recalling it, for in memory neither they nor their love, the heart of my childhood, ever really died.

Hans and Martha, Together

Hans finished his apprenticeship in Haderslev and moved to Fjelstrup to work in the family business. Martha took a job as a nurse-housekeeper for an elderly couple half a mile down the road. The couple lived in an elegant villa such as wealthy farmers built for their retirement when they turned the farms over to sons. The woman was sickly, and young Martha had to sleep in the room with her and attend to her on call at any hour around the clock.

That villa, still beautiful, surrounded by tall trees and modernized, now belongs to my cousin's daughter, Annelie, and her family. Many people have owned the house. One was Doctor Westergård, who proved to be unstable and unlucky, too.

Martha had previously worked in Haderslev at the Railway Hotel, a busy, important place at that time when there were so few cars. Her tutor was an excellent cook, and those skills later helped make the Fjelstrup Inn and Guesthouse known for miles around.

Hans rounded out his education with an eight-month course at an agricultural school, where he learned the skills he needed to run the farm that was part of the inn property.

But this was a time of war, and the couple could not marry. Then one day, Hans simply disappeared. He would have been called into the

German army, and that simply wasn't possible. Hans would not bear arms and wear the uniform of the Germans, Denmark's despised oppressor. What he had done was to escape that fate.

I was twelve or thirteen years old when Father told me about this time in his life as we took a walk. I remember that evening well. It was a rare Denmark night when the wind was still. We did not yet have streetlights, and the darkness fell like velvet.

Father used the time of our walks to tell me many interesting things about the world, but that particular night, I asked him, "Dad, why did you choose Peter Holm to go with you when you rowed across the Lille-Bœlt?" It was a detail about which I had wondered.

His disappearance was a story I had heard something about from my mother. She had received a letter in Hans's handwriting, with a return that said H. Westervang. He had written to say that he was safe, and he had told her about his harrowing boat ride. Of course the change of name was for safety.

Mother told me that he wrote again, urging her to join him and advising her as to strategy. She had to go to the German headquarters and get permission to cross the border into Denmark. Their village, a part of the province of South Jutland, was considered German territory, and they were ruled by German laws.

"I was barely eighteen," she told me, "and a country girl. I was scared, and I kept putting it off." But Hans persisted in his urging, and she finally rode her bike to Haderslev. *I have to do this, I must,* she said to herself. There was no way around it. *This is the day,* she thought. *I am going to do it.*

As it turned out, the German officials were nice enough, asking only a few questions before giving her the permission slip without a fuss. She was so relieved, she hopped on her bike and went right back to Fjelstrup. There she gave notice at her job, and Hans's family helped her to prepare. On a cold, cold day, she got on her bike again with her suitcase and went to the town of Taps. It was so cold that the roads were icy. She made it, though.

I asked her, "Did you take the train from Taps?" We were talking in her cozy living room. She tried to remember, but what was clear to her was that she had to cross two channels—the Lille-Bœlt and then the Store-Bœlt—between Fyen and Sealand. There were no bridges, so she had to go from train to ferry, train to ferry again. Finally she arrived in Roskilde and found Hans waiting for her at the station.

At last they were together again. He was twenty-one, and she eighteen.

Of course Mother's journey was nothing compared to that of Father. He explained to me on that beautiful night why he left and what the crossing was like.

Young men reacted in different ways to their conscription. Some, like Holger Johansen, shot himself in the foot and lost a couple of toes. Some hacked off part of a finger, and some simply fled across the border into Denmark, risking the German border control, who shot such escapees if they saw them.

I knew the story, but not why he had chosen Peter Holm as his companion.

"He wasn't a close friend," Father said. "He was a small man and not strong, but his father had a woodworking shop, they lived close to the beach, and they owned a rowboat! So you see, I talked to Peter. He wasn't all that eager to go, because he was smitten with a girl named Ella, but he didn't want to lose his life in the German army either, so he agreed, reluctantly."

They planned to row to an island called Brandsø. It lies midway between South Jutland and the island of Fyen, but is still in Danish territory. There were some farms on that small island, and they hoped to find shelter there while awaiting further transport.

They planned the trip together carefully. They told no one, not even Ella (Peter's girl) or Martha. On a dark fall night, they shoved the boat from shore and started pulling the oars. They had to reach Brandsø before daylight or risk discovery by German patrol boats.

Father continued his story. "In the beginning we did well, but after a couple of hours of hard rowing, we realized that the strong currents had taken us off our course and past Brandsø. Peter was beginning to fold. Our hands were blistered. We had brought beer and bread, and that helped, but panic set in when Peter stood up to relieve himself and his oar floated away.

"I was frantic and furious. Peter never really forgave me for cursing him as I did," Father said quietly. "It was wrong of me—he didn't do it on purpose, after all. But rowing with one oar was useless. We hung over the edge and paddled frantically with our arms."

I could imagine the awful sense of dread and defeat he must have felt that night. "We continued paddling with all our might, and then, miraculously, we began to see some faint lights on the horizon. The single oar could be used again when the water got shallow enough to reach bottom. We pushed with all our strength till we reached shore."

They had reached land before daylight, but they were far from safe. They had hoped to reach Fyen. In the strong current, they might have drifted back into German territory. They really didn't know where they were.

As we walked in the dark night, Father paused, his hand holding mine in his pocket. I sensed that he was far away as he continued. "We hid the boat as well as we could on the beach and started walking through fields, avoiding roads. We came to a farm and heard cows, so we knew that someone could soon come to milk. We were terribly cold in wet clothes and boots, so we buried ourselves in straw in the barn. Soon we heard voices.

"Oh, little girl," he said to me, his voice shaking slightly. "I had never been so happy as I was at the moment I heard those voices speaking Danish with the lilting dialect of Fyen. We stayed in our straw heap a bit longer, listening, resting. When the milking was about done, we came out of hiding and told the farmer of our plight.

"Even though we had rowed twenty-five to thirty miles, the farmer did not seem surprised. He told us that other young men had come the same way. The farmer and his family fed us and dried our clothes while we slept, but after that they expected us to move on. That was all right. We had what we wanted: our freedom and our lives."

Peter stayed on that island and found work in a woodworking shop. My father traveled to Roskilde, near Copenhagen. He worked on a farm and then found work as a guard or warden in an institution for the poor and homeless. It was run by a couple called Oscar and Gerda Christiansen, who were to become lifelong friends of our family.

When Martha arrived in Roskilde, Hans took her to Oscar and Gerda. They were very concerned for these young people from South Jutland, and they had opened their home to others.

My parents named my sister after Gerda Christiansen, and the families stayed in close touch. Many years later, my mother stayed with the Christiansens to recover when she was attacked by a cow and suffered a nervous breakdown.

Martha soon found a housekeeper's job with a Doctor Gravesen and stayed there for over a year. She wanted to improve her skills, though, so she went on to a large estate south of Roskilde. That estate is called Holmegard, and later it became well-known for the high quality glassware produced there. Martha, though so young, had the responsibility for a large kitchen and other staff. Long afterward, telling me about it, I sensed her pride in that.

Then, in 1918, the horrible war was over, the German army was defeated, and those in exile, like Hans and Martha, could cross the border and go home. Mother said that the lady of the estate hated to see her go, but of course she and Hans were eager to return to their families.

Yet it would be two more years before they could marry. My grandparents, Elise and Søren Wilhelm Petersen, had to wait for their house to be built so that they could move and make room for the young couple.

And there were two years of wrangling and politics before the plebiscite took place that brought South Jutland back to Denmark. So many German citizens had infiltrated the province, they held a majority in the towns of Flensborg, Kiel, and Slesvig. But at last, on July 10, 1920, the Danish King Christian X rode a white horse across the border into United Denmark. Thousands of red and white flags, some of them hastily sewn from tablecloths or bedspreads, were hung from newly erected flagpoles. Any way they could, the Danish people decked themselves out in Danish colors all across the country. To the grieving Danes left behind, the King promised, "You shall not be forgotten."

And to this day, in every church in Denmark, on every Sunday, people pray for those Danes who were left below the border.

But this was a happy time for Martha and Hans, who set their wedding date for May 28, 1920. They began their life together in the inn. Eight long years had gone by since they met at a dancing party in Haderslev. Martha was twenty-four and Hans was twenty-seven.

I have a photograph of them standing in the garden on their wedding day. Martha is in a makeshift gown made by her mother. She is carrying a

Above: King Christian X crossing the border on July 10, 1920.

Left: Plebiscite proclamation, 1920.

Hans and Martha Petersen.

bouquet of flowers scrounged from the early spring garden. Hans is in his father's formal suit. It isn't just the radiance of their enduring love that makes this picture so special, but also the exuberance of celebrating their wedding day in a free country, in a small town blanketed in the Danish flag of red and white.

There were many good years in that inn, and we three children, all born in the upstairs bedroom, had a good life. I recall many happy times, and over the years, have recollected them far more than I have the difficult ones. I think that is the right balance, but it is important to honor my parents by remembering them fully. Now I understand how hard they had to struggle, through Depression years, through family troubles, through hard work, late hours, curtailed privacy. In time, the labor and strain took a toll on our mother, making her vulnerable when she was traumatized by the cow's attack, and she could not fully recover from her breakdown while we continued to live at the inn. Somehow Father got enough money together to purchase the house and dry goods business across the street. Andreas Nielsen had succumbed to the Depression and had had to leave. Father was trained as a businessman, and somehow he was able to convince the wealthiest store owner in the area, Mr. Hundevat in Haderslev, to put his faith in him and stake him to enough inventory to stock the shelves.

A new concept was thus born—a satellite store, the first of its kind, I believe. Certainly it was the first in Fjelstrup.

The years passed happily for me, and for Willy and Gerda, too, as children, but the time came when we had to make our own lives.

Childhood became the past, and I began a new life.

The town choir—important people in Fjelstrup:

Back row: Peter Jepsen (teacher), Otto Zielke (saddlemaker), Christian Jorgensen (farmer), Jorgen Friis (farmer, county official), Herman Rohard (uncle), Jes Hansen (farmer), Claus Hobner (farmer), Andor Møller (baker, mayor), Emil Have (farmer), Carl Hollesen (blacksmith).

Middle row: Johanne Olsen (housewife, shoemaker's wife), Grete Petersen ("Old Grete," spinster), Frie Jorgensen (homeschool teacher, From family), Dagmar Nilsen (wife of Andreas Nilsen), Johanne Larsen (wife of Laurits Larsen), Jørgen From (farmer), Jeppe Friss (farmer).

Bottom row: Anne Jepsen (wife of teacher Peter Jepsen), Marie Christensen (wife of tailor Christensen), Musse Have (wife of Emil Have), Anna Schov (spinster), Marie Bramsen (widow—the self-ordained godmother), Martha Petersen (my mother), Anna Cornett (telephone lady), Marie Petersen (aunt, wife of Jokum Petersen), Miss Petersen (teacher).

Snowy Night

They lay on the snow
three little girls
with boots and red caps
coats made of wool
no sound was heard
from the sledding hill
voices and laughter,
loud and shrill
gone silent and still.

The wild boys went their way
pushing and shoving
dragging their sleigh,
leaving footprints and spit
on the snow behind.

The three little girls
stayed quietly behind
found a spot
by the willow tree
with blankets of snow
smooth and cool
sparkling with frosty glitter.

They laughed as they fell
flat on their backs
on that blanket of crunchy white.
The world so still,
they dared not talk
as the moonface watched them
through whispery clouds.

WINTER 1932, DENMARK

Who Do We See?

Do we see the mother
with the thick brown hair
is that her
in the high-back chair
Her eyes are the same
the voice—a little frail
her back got bent
but the smile is the same,
the face has wrinkles
framed by angel hair.

She talks to us
her two old girls
recalls memories
from long long ago.

When she laughs like that
telling her stories
about visiting her Grandpa
the one who snores
and Grandma's dumplings
so heavy and tough,
we laugh with her,
we giggle with glee
who is it then,
who do we see

The pretty young girl
with the thick brown hair.
—It's her sitting there
in the high-back chair

Sing Happy Songs for Me

for my mother, Martha

Who spoke to me,
gently broke my sleep
a touch so soft,
a whisper in my ear,
a gentle brush
like a mother's kiss
touched upon my cheek.

Why did I wake,
the night is barely waning
the first rays of daylight
just past the sill
muted strands of bird song
sounding far away
greeting this new day.

Who can it be
my mind began to ponder
I am not alone
I am warm
I rested well,
secure and safe
in my family home.

The phone is heard
it rang from far away
I clearly understood.

It was my mother's touch
the gentle kiss,
the whisper in my ear.
It was her spirit
come to tell me this.

I am on my way
daughter dear
I will be with Dad
all will be well
I am ready now
I lived so long
I must leave you here.

Do not fret
cry or worry
just one last thing I ask
when you come home
to say farewell
and when you sit
inside the church
Sing only happy songs for me,
I loved you all so well.

We went to see her
resting in the chapel
a smile was on her face
her hands held yellow daffodils.

She had not left
inside of us she lived
her voice was silent
but as she'd asked
we now would sing
the songs she sang
the words she knew
songs of spring and jubilation
the sun through leaded windowpanes
pays tribute to the mother
we knew and loved so well.

Visit on a Summer Night

The sun sets late in my Nordic land
the bells have long since rung
It must be half past ten at least
dusky shadows wrap the town
in soft and muted light.
No sound is heard, save for a faint voice
or two, coming from the inn.
Good night they say, be safe,
Good night again, the gravel crunch
under wheels as they drive away.

Now all is still; as a ghostly shadow
I softly haunt the lanes,
in that faintest light I see it all
the way it was before I left my home,
before the lanes were paved,
before the streets had sidewalks
and were marked with names.

I pass by the preacher's house
hidden in the trees,
across the way, around the church I see
the sturdy wall they built,
Andreas and his son called Svend.
They worked for days and months
fitting stone by stone
each against the other,
cemented carefully.

A work of art it was,
of love and dedication,
for uncounted years it'll surely stand
to safeguard the folks from town
who lie beneath the tower
of the old white church,
Andreas and Svend among them.

The iron gate creaks a bit
when I step inside the wall,
I close it carefully and make my way
on the narrow paths between the graves.
They are all there, the folks I knew so well,
markers tell their names,
the years they lived, when they died,
their families around them,
each plot lovingly attended
with wreaths and flowers in metal vases.

On the path along the way
I spot that little stone.
It was more than sixty years
since Chresten died.
He caught a cold,
his lungs got sick,
the church bells sadly tolled
that day his life had come to end.

We kids from school
strewed flowers in his path,
as the stately black hearse,
with fringe and crepe,
drawn by shiny horses,
took Chresten from his home.
Inside the church we sang and prayed,
we cried our tears,
then laid him down to rest
beneath that small white stone.

We thought of him, the quiet kid
quite ordinary,
living at the edge of town
where no one really knew him.
But through our pain,
our sorrow and regret
he achieved a higher status.

Like a hero,
he fought and lost,
and earned a special place.

I grew old, I saw the world
he stayed there in his grave
just eight years old,
a little boy, too young to die.
But on my visit,
in the dusky summer night,
I stop to think and wonder,
what might have come of him
if he had only lived.

His stone, once so pure and white
is broken, his name almost obscured
by moss and wind and rain and time
but still—I see it there,
—Sleep well, dear little Chresten—
is what it says,
sleep well throughout the years.

FJELSTRUP, DENMARK

2

FIVE BITTER YEARS
Living under German Occupation

Invasion: 1940

In 1940 I was a schoolgirl of fifteen, just beyond my childhood innocence, still looking to my parents to gauge the world. During the Depression, they had worried and I had not. Having fewer material things was insignificant to me; our family had love and security, and very little about my life then depended on money. I was, however, encouraged to read the papers and listen to the twice-daily newscast beamed at us from Copenhagen. I was aware of the increasing tension below our border, and I understood enough of the German language to grasp the hysteria in Hitler's rabble-rousing speeches that cluttered the airwaves every Sunday afternoon. I heard the thrilled excitement in the thousands of voices cheering him on as they chanted, Sieg Heil! I could not ignore Father's expression as he leaned close to listen to the radio on those Sunday afternoons. I saw his worry, too, as he discussed the situation with friends and neighbors. As I watched my parents react, I too was unsettled.

They had known the bitterness of German domination all too well. Since the war of 1864, for fifty-seven tedious years, throughout their childhood and youth, our province of South Jutland had been ruled by German laws. It had been twenty years since my parents stood in front of the old inn with the red and white flags waving in the sun under a clear blue sky, celebrating the retreat of the Germans, the end of a war, and the return of our province to Denmark. Now all of that was threatened.

Mother tried to console Father. "But Hans, we have an agreement with Germany," she reminded him. "They promised never to cross our borders again." I'm sure she sought comfort in saying that, but she, like Father, surely sensed danger. Our small village was only fifty kilometers (thirty-five miles) from their border. Copenhagen, our capital, located on the island of Zealand, just across the channel from Sweden, was as far away from us as one can get in Denmark.

As if they had never been defeated, Germany strutted and marched across Europe.

Starting in 1939, German troops swiftly barged through Poland, and in short order proceeded to occupy Austria, Romania, Hungary, and Czechoslovakia. It was true that both Denmark and Norway had neutrality agreements with Germany, but there was no real confidence that Germany would honor them. And as we would learn all too soon, the Germans had meticulously scouted harbors and made their careful plans. Troops had been assembled at the border less than fifty kilometers south of our town of Fjelstrup.

Even as we dreaded the inevitable, even when they marched across our border and invaded our whole country within a few hours on the morning of April 9, 1940, we couldn't really know just how terrible the war years would be for us. On the day that Germany invaded us, our lives opened to a staggering, bewildering, and tragic time. Every town and village of our small nation was snatched from rightful government within a few hours. Denmark is a small, flat country, and as one Danish soldier said, "We didn't even have a decent place to hide." When Norway was invaded on the very same day, they were protected by mountains and narrow fjords, and they put up a fight that lasted for several weeks and cost Germany dearly.

Days after the invasion of Denmark, the same fate befell Holland and Belgium. Then France, Yugoslavia, Bulgaria, and Greece fell to the German army. The Germans would not falter until they marched into Russia in June of 1941. Despite troops in Egypt and North Africa and all of the European countries I have mentioned, Germany weakened in 1941 in the face of Russia's vastness and terrible winter. Nevertheless, their aggression would continue for years yet to come.

With shocking, speedy efficiency, the invaders took over the airwaves and began broadcasting their propaganda and instructions. They told us that we were safe and that no harm would come to us if we followed their orders. They actually told us they had come to protect us from English invasion!

It seemed no more than an instant until our lives, and our hearts, were plunged into darkness. First, we were ordered to cover all windows with dark shades so that no light could escape. Soldiers would patrol the streets, and if they saw light, the family would be issued a warning, once, and after that, a stiff fine. Also, for the next five years no light shone in our streets! Not only did we walk in darkness, but we were also kept in the dark in a worse way, cut off from all information about what was happening in the rest of Denmark. We would not know until the war was over about the atrocities committed in Copenhagen and about our beloved king's courageous actions against Hitler and the German occupation.

By 1940, my family was no longer living in the Fjelstrup Inn. Mother's health had suffered and my father had taken over the dry goods store across the street, where we also lived. From there we could see the soldiers moving about in the inn we knew so well, a place of so much liveliness and communal spirit: weddings, funerals, meetings, dances. My father's sister, Hanne, and her husband, Herman, had taken over the inn, and they were permitted to live in the private quarters of the building.

April was the start of spring, and, as always, it passed gently into summer, but no one seemed to notice the freshness and the beauty of our beech tree forests or the white anemones mixed with purple violets that carpeted the forest floor. Usually spring was a semi-sacred time after our long, dark winter nights and the months of few daylight hours. It was a time for long walks beneath the pale green leafy canopy, a time of joy and happiness when our song and laughter mingled with that of the birdsong and the rare sounds of the elusive cuckoo bird. Summer did come, of course, but our usual activities held little appeal. Who could splash in salt waves on the broad beaches when our precious land was blanketed in grief and sorrow? For the first time—indeed, it was the only time—I saw my strong father cry in despair. As a young man in World War I, subject to conscription in the German army, he had bravely escaped, returning when the threat was gone and our province was once again a part of

Denmark. And of course both Mother and Father well remembered their childhood, when they had had to attend German schools, sing German songs, and abide by German rules. The day in 1920 when South Jutland was reunited with motherland Denmark and King Christian X rode across the border on his stately white horse had been a day of celebration, relief, and optimism.

Now, the Germans were back, and there was no escape, for there was no free territory in Denmark. Even our private homes were violated. After a few months, two officers went from house to house to see how many people occupied each. In our case, we had three bedrooms, but since my brother, Willy, had finished his apprenticeship and left home, there was an empty room. My parents were notified that two German soldiers would shortly move into the spare room.

There was nothing we could do to prevent this, but our father sat Gerda and me down to prepare us. We were never to face these men, he told us. We were never to speak to them. We were to listen for their movement, and avoid them, no matter how this inconvenienced us.

To this day, when I tell people that Gerda and I slept in the room right next to the room where two German soldiers were housed, but we never once saw their faces or spoke to them, I have to explain how it was possible. Our house had a separate entrance hall with doors leading into all the different rooms; this was the custom in Europe. The floor was red slate tile, and the stairs were uncarpeted. As a result, it was easy to hear the soldiers as they approached. Their studded boots rang out on the tiles as they threw open the front door and stomped up the bare staircase.

As winter approached and the days again grew short, we began to pick up our lives and to try to adjust to the omnipresent soldiers. We ignored the harsh sounds of their language and the ever-present trampling sounds of their boots. We managed to adjust to each new indignity that was forced on us. We went about our everyday duties of school and work. We were issued ID cards with our pictures on them, and we had to carry them on us at all times. We picked up ration books and got used to dwindling store supplies. We had always imported our luxury goods, and now such foods as oranges, lemons, almonds, and spices were absent. I did not know that I would not taste a banana or a piece of chocolate again for five years.

Mother's ID card.

Some people hoarded yard goods made from cotton and wool, but eventually things ran out and substitutions began to appear. Willy had completed his four-year apprenticeship as a tailor, and he opened a small shop in my parents' house for a time. With no cloth from which to make suits, he ripped up old suits and overcoats. He cleaned and pressed the pieces, turned them inside out, and fashioned new garments for customers. From two dark blue coats that Gerda and I had outgrown he made me one of the best-fitting jackets I have ever owned. We also unraveled old sweaters and washed the yarn, then fashioned it into new, multicolored creations. My mother took apart the black dress she had worn for her civil wedding service, and she made a lovely dress for Gerda with it. I didn't have Gerda's luck. My white confirmation dress was dyed dark red, truly ugly to say the least, and that was my best "going-out" dress.

All around us, people were ingenious and patient, focused on solving the new problems that faced us all, but Grandmother Anne Sofie especially impressed me. She quietly spent hours and hours knitting soles for our worn-out socks and sewed them onto the old socks. She never complained. That the bottoms did not match the tops of the socks didn't matter; they were warm and whole. As Gerda and I sat on the floor near her, she told us stories from the many books she had read.

Food was a problem. Coffee drinkers roasted rye grain to brew an evil-tasting drink. Dried apple leaves became our "tea," and other leaves were used to make smelly, foul-tasting cigarettes. We got them in packages of five and smoked them down so far that we had to hold them with a bobby pin to get that last awful drag. Our sugar ration was 125 grams (about ¼ pound) per month. Since butter, bacon, and other agricultural products were Denmark's main export items, you would think we might at least have enjoyed those things, but the German army needed our food. We could not get margarine or other oil products except for one stick of butter a month and maybe a little lard.

The food, we were told, was partial payment for the Germans' "protection." After all, they were *Das Vernemact*, keeping us safe from the evil English.

Daily Life

Still, the church bell rang each morning and rang again at sundown, as it had done for countless years. People went about their tasks. Peter Holm, the milkman, passed from house to house sounding his bell. He measured milk and buttermilk into the pitchers and bowls set out by housewives. There was no cream, and for butter he had to count ration stamps. Hans Madsen, the mailman, donned his red coat and rode his bike through the village, delivering mail. Days rolled into weeks, then months, and we had to submit to each change and restriction forced upon us by the foreign army.

In our house we spent the winter months in Father's office. During the day the store was heated, but in the evening, that tiny room was the only warm place in the house. When, on very special and rare occasions, our mother heated the living room, we felt as if we were invited guests. In the office, a small upright stove with a little oven near the top stood in the corner. My sister and I heated two bricks in it each evening, and after supper we wrapped them in newspaper and put them in our beds. Our parents each had a hot water bottle (actually an oval metal contraption with a screw-top) that they filled with hot water.

Our room was icy, and we loved that warm spot in our beds as we crawled in! The heavy featherbeds were damp. The room was damp. There was no insulation, and on cold nights we could see frost glistening on the walls. We wormed our way down toward the heaven-sent bricks to warm our feet through our knitted socks.

Our German "protectors" took all the coal and benzene (gasoline) for their war machine. All cars were put up on blocks. We walked or rode our bicycles, unless we were lucky enough to squeeze onto the bus that passed through town two times a day. That was no easy task, since soldiers rode, too, pushing and shoving.

For heat, we burned peat dug up from the ancient bogs around us. There were large digging fields, and some of the dried peat was fairly decent fuel while the weather held out, but we could not count on Danish summers, known for their intermittent wind and rain, and much of our fuel was wet. Burning it was a messy affair. It sizzled and steamed brown juice that ran from the bottom of the stove into a pan Mother had wisely placed beneath.

Once in a while we listened to a radio-play or a concert, but the Germans generally filled the air with propaganda, and at that, Father turned the radio off promptly. He loved to read, so he often sat in the chair next to his desk with a book. Mother, who didn't read, spent her time knitting or mending, and Gerda and I sat at a little table by a bookcase and did homework.

Sometimes we played cards or board games, but without fail, promptly at 8:30, Gerda and I had to go out into the freezing kitchen and fix the

evening coffee. We hated doing it, and tried to ignore it, but Mom would remind us, or Father would give us a look that got us going.

Danes have to have coffee in the evening, even if it tastes awful, even if the cakes to eat with it are dry and tasteless as sawdust.

Since Mother cooked our meals on two hotplates, the kitchen was icy. Gerda and I complained and argued over who would leave the warm office first. It never occurred to us to take turns. Neither of us would have been able to bear the thought of the other cozily warm while one of us suffered in the frigid kitchen! Misery loves company. Now I realize that our parents' efforts to make our lives run as normally as possible, honoring our usual rituals, kept us from despair.

Not everyone lived such a chilly life as ours. Across the street, two German officers assigned to our Uncle Jokum's house were more or less welcomed for the sake of the comforts they could bring. Aunt Marie, too spacey to realize how she sounded, sometimes gushed cheerfully that the officers brought real coffee, tobacco, and even vintage cognac to the household.

I can only imagine how much our parents and neighbors resented this, but no one spoke of it front of Gerda and me. It is a sad and mysterious puzzle how the invasion of the German army could have divided our family so. Many other families and neighbors were similarly stretched thin to understand one another, and later, to forgive. After all, some among us were informers, for some neighbors simply and suddenly disappeared, never to be heard from again. Few complained about our hardships, but there was real danger, something else altogether.

Tension between the invaders and the Danish people grew more hostile, harsh and dangerous. By late 1942, buildings that had been taken over by the Germans were being sabotaged—even precious old university halls and other important structures. The underground movement became stronger, better organized, and more effective. None of us knew who belonged, just as we didn't know who were the spies who told the Germans what they knew. Only after the war could traitors be identified and punished. That my own brother played an active part in the underground would be news to me, for if we had known during the occupation, we would have been in great danger in case we were interrogated. Willy's group, we learned later,

Hanne and Herman on their wedding day.

hid weapons in the anteroom of the old church and participated in many forays unknown to us.

The worst of our relationships was within our own family. My father's sister, Hanne, had married a handsome, charming German whose name, ironically, was Herman (the German). He had become a Danish citizen after South Jutland rejoined Denmark in 1920, with the sponsorship of my father and his best friend, Laurits Larsen. Herman joined in family affairs and behaved as a responsible citizen. He was a member of the same choir as Mother, adding his strong voice, and he often played the lead in plays at the inn. Of course we cousins played together. We were family.

But Uncle Herman changed under the strain of the occupation. Perhaps it was Hitler's rabble-rousing speeches on the radio. Perhaps it was the hysteria brought on by the sounds of German marching songs, played constantly on the radio and broadcast into our streets. In any case, Herman was overcome in the frenzy, and when he was offered a good position in the construction of a German airfield being built

Hanne sewing a Danish flag.

in a farmer's field near the town of Vojens, thirty kilometers to the south, he took it and became a part of the Nazi movement that had robbed us of our freedom.

No one spoke of it in my presence. I remember him arriving on the bus, well-dressed and loaded with packages for his family. From the airfield job he was moved to one in Copenhagen. I don't know what he did there. He came home for visits, but for the rest of the war years, he worked where the Germans sent him.

Indirectly, through him I learned a valuable lesson. After the war was over he was arrested by the Danish government and jailed for assisting the enemy. I don't know how long he was away, as I left home during that time. I think it must have been about a year, because when I came home for Mother's fiftieth birthday celebration on August 4, 1946, he had been home for a short while.

After the sad war years, we were eager to celebrate. People from both sides of the family were invited to our home. I heard my parents considering whether to invite Herman. We were at the dinner table when Father said decisively, "I am going over to see Herman and ask him to the party." I was surprised. I knew Father hated everything German, but he went on to say, "Herman is my sister's husband. We have to live together as a family. The war is over, and this is a good time for him to get back in the fold."

I learned later that Herman protested, feeling too ashamed to face the people he had betrayed, but Father convinced him that he had to make the step. He didn't come

Lisse and Egon

84

for dinner, but when Willy started playing his harmonica and we were dancing in the front hall on the red tile floor, the door opened slowly just enough for Herman to squeeze through.

Willy kept playing. We kept dancing. No one spoke. Then Father went to Herman, shook his hand, and spoke loudly enough for all to hear. "Welcome back," he said. "We are glad you came." And he steered him in to meet everyone.

I was so proud of my father, and so glad to have Uncle Herman back in the family. How good it was to see Aunt Hanne and cousins Lisse and Egon happy again. How right it was that the anger and tension were gone.

From my father, I learned how to forgive and get on with life.

Jokum and Marie

As our lives adjusted, so did the lives of our friends and neighbors and relatives. In the family of Jokum, my father's brother, and his wife, Marie, however, tension and tragedy had been building for years. During the occupation they increasingly isolated themselves. We had little contact with them and were left wondering what really went on within the walls of the elegant gray brick villa across from us.

Jokum Petersen, like my father, Hans, had worked as an apprentice in an area business, the accepted way that young men received their training. Besides the apprenticeship of four years, during which they learned the details of running a business, the two brothers also attended a trade school and took appropriate courses in retail and wholesale transactions, along with courses in language and math. They received room and board but very little pay. When all requirements were completed, they received a certificate stating that they had the necessary skills to run a business.

All of this was preparation for the day the two boys would take over the family conglomerate: a grocery and farm supply store, the inn, farmland, barns, and livestock. When Jokum chose the grocery and supply business, my father took some agricultural courses to extend his knowledge of farming. When he married my mother in 1920, they took over that part of the business. A house was built for the Petersen grandparents at the east end of the property, just beyond the dance hall and garden. The grandparents' income would derive from the two family enterprises.

Jokum was slim and fair-haired, with a narrow, feline face. Small of stature, he nevertheless seemed tall because of his straight, almost elegant bearing. He could be very charming and outgoing with customers, but it's doubtful that anyone really knew him well. He guarded his privacy with a vengeance. In all the years I knew him, I cannot recall a single meaningful conversation between us, nor did he ever inquire about my life and well-being.

Nevertheless, the store prospered under his skillful leadership. He was innovative in drawing in customers, and when cars became more common, he added a gas pump in the front, the kind with a handle that pulled back and forth, filling up two glass cylinders. Each cylinder held five liters of gasoline, and when they were pumped full, the gas was released into the hose leading to the automobile tank. It fascinated me to see the gas rise in the cylinders, and as often as I could, I ran out to watch. Jokum seldom worked the pump unless someone very important came along. He had a helper, or later, my Aunt Marie, do it.

He was one of the few people who had a telephone, and in his office adjoining the store, he had a typewriter. I often went in there with my father, but I was not allowed to touch the typewriter, and I never saw Jokum use it. He had a big safe, where I suppose he kept his money. He was certainly much better off than my father, and he drove one of the fanciest cars in town. I remember that my father had a Model-T Ford with an oval window in back, and when he got a newer model with a square window, he showed it to Jokum with great pride, but Jokum was unimpressed. During the Depression years, Jokum hired my father to deliver grocery orders to the outlying farms on a weekly basis. Usually Gerda and I went along. We loved the trip, and we loved it when housewives offered us cookies and juice.

Inside the grocery store there was a large U-shaped counter and two side counters with glass fronts for displays. On the right were special items such as china, glasses, and bowls. Jokum also had some kitchen utensils and a few gift items such as hand mirrors and comb and brush sets. I very clearly remember receiving some of those things for my confirmation. I was given only the comb and hairbrush, and when I later saw the matching hand mirror in the case, my uncle asked me if I wished to buy it! My parents were so angered by his stinginess they would not let me get it.

The counter on the left held cigars and cigarettes, pipes, little scissors to trim the ends of cigars, and of course many kinds of tobacco, snuff, and chew tobacco. Another glass case held candy bars. Regular hard candies were stored in big glass jars in front of the case. There were no plastic bags then, but Jokum or Marie would twist a square of parchment paper into a tight cone that we called a *tut*. It was a rare treat to receive a tut filled with candy, weighed carefully on the scale according to how much money we had. Our uncle was not generous with us.

A bell hung above the entrance door and sounded when anyone entered or left the store. A big coffee-mill with two large silver wheels and a fancy bowl on top with a lid sat in the window at the end of the cigar case. When someone ordered coffee, the beans were weighed on a scale and then poured into the bowl, and the machine was turned on. The wheels spun round and round, the silver surfaces shining brightly and the smell of freshly ground coffee filling the air.

Coffee was a very important item. Housewives would shop at the store they felt had the best coffee. Jokum ordered green beans by the sackful. In a shed out back, he roasted them himself in a large rotating drum. A coal fire beneath provided the heat, and he turned the crank slowly and evenly until the beans took on just the right color. He trusted no one else to do the job, though he would let me watch as long as I did not talk.

Behind the counter the long wall was covered with shelves and many drawers of various sizes. The shelves held bottles and jars of cinnamon sticks, whole vanilla beans, many kinds of spices, and other fascinating items. Stored under the counter were big barrels of flour and sugar, oatmeal, rice, and the jelly-like green soap housewives used for cleaning. Everything was measured or weighed according to the orders of the customers.

All the eggs and produce brought in by farmers were kept in the large barn attached to the store. Big bins held coal and coke used for heating and cooking. Jokum had a hired man who managed that department. In the store he usually had a clerk and an apprentice to help him.

In time, one of those clerks was a sixteen-year-old girl called Marie. She came from a neighboring town, from a large, rather poor family that had difficulties making ends meet. It's easy to understand how she was quite bowled over by the good fortune of being hired to work in Jokum's grocery store. Her job enabled her to escape her drab home and the many household chores and childcare she had to do there to help her mother. All of a sudden she was in a place full of people, of action! She took to it like a duck to water, and quickly became well-liked by customers.

Marie.

Despite the fact that she was deathly afraid of Jokum, she was swept away by his cool charm. He was her boss, a man of thirty, fourteen years her senior. It is not surprising that Jokum intimidated her into an affair, and soon she was pregnant with his child.

The family flew into an uproar, but Grandmother Elise asserted a will stronger than her son's. She insisted that Jokum marry Marie to protect the family name. She did consider Marie and her family below the Petersens on the social ladder, but she was carrying Jokum's child, and marry her he did!

They built a new house of light gray brick on the north end of the property. Jokum could afford a nice house, one that was bigger and better-appointed than most in town. Young Marie moved into this nice house, but she faced a lifetime of servitude to a man who neither loved nor respected her.

The child was soon born, a son they named Erik. I am told he was strong and healthy, but after a beach outing, he caught a cold and died of pneumonia. He was less than a year old.

Two other children were born, a girl named Elise (Lise), and a boy called William. Many years later another boy was born, also called Erik.

Jokum set the tone for the family and Marie catered to his every whim. The children learned at an early age not to let anyone into their home and lives.

As the children matured, seeds of tragedy began to grow slowly in Jokum's family. The girl Elise went to the town of Haderslev to apprentice with a photographer. She led a shiftless life, and even though my sister tried to be friendly with her cousin, Gerda was left with the task of telling Elise to resign from the sports club in which both of them were active. By this time Denmark was occupied by the German army, and members of the club had seen Elise in the company of despised enemy soldiers. Later in her life, she bore two children by unknown fathers.

The son William was my age. Like his father, he was skillful in business matters, and he was destined to take over the family store. Some major test of wills must have occurred, because William suddenly left the village and was soon named manager of an auto dealership in Haderslev. Jokum, true to his nature, acted as if nothing had happened, but when William later died in an automobile accident just two months after he married his high school sweetheart, some signs of desperation emerged in this ironclad man. He lashed out at the grief-stricken bride and demanded that she return all the wedding gifts she had received from her dead husband's family.

My father, Hans, tried to enter his brother's house of pain, but he was not allowed in. William's grieving mother, Marie, filled the rooms of their

home with pictures of him, pictures from every age; they were on every wall and on every piece of furniture. William was buried in a cemetery in Haderslev, as the young widow wished. And life went on.

William and Lise.

As the years went by, the wounds seemed to heal. But the family's suffering was not over. During the Nazi occupation, the German soldiers were frequent customers at the store. Marie, in her silent desperation, her suppressed grief and despair, sought and received attention from them. She spoke German well, so she was able to flirt with them, to understand as they flattered her. They made her feel young, attractive, and popular. Soon she became pregnant and gave birth to a healthy, robust redheaded little boy. He was the second Erik. Rumors and gossip engulfed the village.

Although stunned, neighbor women brought food and gifts according to custom, and everybody waited. But nothing happened. Jokum remained hidden behind his shield of privacy, and went on with his life. As the child grew, Jokum's health began to fail. Slowly sickness and pain took over his body and ravished him, but from his room in the back of the house, he still managed to tyrannize Marie with constant demands through the days and nights.

My father visited and offered comfort, but no one else from the village stopped at his door. He died in his damp little room in the back of the house. Few people came to the funeral service. He was not buried next to his parents in the family plot by the church. Instead, he was buried in Haderslev, next to his son, as he had ordered.

Marie lived her days alone in her elegant house, abandoned even by her daughter, Elise, and yes, by the redheaded son as well.

Dad, Mom, and Jokum.

Harvest

During summer my parents sent me to nearby farms to help with the harvest and with household chores. My memories of those summers are a mix of emotions. I hated getting up before six every morning, having to clean chicken houses, put new straw in the nests, and set out food and water. I had to do all this before helping the farm wife fix breakfast for the men who would be coming in from milking.

At that time there were no milking machines, tractors, or other technology to ease the labor of the farmer. There wasn't even running water in the barn or the house. Bathing facilities consisted of a bucket with water and a wash basin in our room. The outhouse was in one of the barns, and it was very painful for me to walk there with the eyes of the farmhands on me, knowing full well where I was headed.

On the other hand, I loved being part of the team that brought in the sheaves of oats, barley, and wheat with the horses and wagons. The experienced men packed the wagon evenly and solidly to keep it from tipping on the way home. Loading the wagon and throwing the bundles up into the barn loft for storage was enormously hard work. We rested after noon dinner for an hour, and during the afternoon, the farm wife brought coffee and bread out to us in the field. Getting the harvest inside the barn was of utmost importance, given the unpredictability of Danish summer weather.

In hindsight, I have come to appreciate those grueling summer jobs. All of us on the farm were a team with a common goal. Certainly we ached at the end of the day, but there was no time for whining. The sun still shone at eight or nine as we piled into bed. Exhausted, we didn't think about the war raging around us. We came to take for granted the pulsating sounds of engines as British planes flew their missions over us, headed for the industrial cities of Germany. The air raid sirens would sound, but we slept on, no basement to go to and too tired to care.

When the British planes were chased by the German *Messerschmitts*, our circumstances beneath them were more serious. For one thing, when in danger, the Brits might drop unnecessary ballast, such as small firebombs. They were round cylinders with red ends about a foot long. We were warned not to touch them. Usually the German police appeared to pick them up. One night, though, a larger bomb was dropped in a field just below our farm, making a deep muffled sound and shaking the old farmhouse.

When we went down the next morning to see the field, I was surprised that there were no mounds of dirt piled up, only a large, round hole. The soft earth had just compacted; I heard the farmer wondering how he would find enough soil to fill it up.

In 1944, long after I had left the farm, it happened that an English airplane on a bombing mission in Germany was shot down only a few kilometers away from where I had spent my summer. On a dark February evening it got caught in the crossfire of German fighter planes. It fell in the nearby woods called Avnø and was quickly engulfed in flames. There were seven men aboard, but only one escaped.

Years later, my friend Vagn Rasmussen told me about his experience:

During the air raid my parents and I were sitting in the barn behind the horse stalls. They were made of solid cement, and my father figured it was as good and safe a place as anywhere. The Germans had ordered every household that did not have a basement to dig a shelter, but my strong-willed father was not about to sit in a hole in the ground.

Through the windows in the barn we could see the flames from the fallen plane shooting into the sky. The Gestapo came within the hour and cordoned off the whole area. With the curfew strictly enforced, it was not until morning that my friend Axel and I decided to do some scouting around. We knew those woods and fields like the palms of our hands, and we managed to get fairly close. We could not get to the burned-out wreck because of the German soldiers, but we sneaked across the narrow farm road nearby. Suddenly we saw a dead flyer lying on the ground. He was all yellow in his face and it made a terrible impression on me. I was only ten years old and I had never seen a dead person before. After he was taken away, we could still see the imprint of his body in the soft, swampy soil. Years later, after the war had ended, some parents came to visit the place where their sons had perished.

Later we heard about the one flyer who escaped, how he was found and helped by some young men who under the cover of darkness defied the Germans and roamed the fields. They led him to a place called

Sillerupgård. He had lost one of his boots, but they helped him along. One reason they took him to that particular farm was that the lady, Mrs. Frederiksen, spoke English. She took him in and fed him breakfast. After a nap on the sofa and a hot bath, she had him write letters to his family in Canada and his girlfriend in England. But it was clear that she had no way of keeping him or hiding him. The Gestapo soon pulled up with an armed truck loaded with SS troops.

As upset as Mrs. Frederiksen was, she hugged and kissed the young flyer right in front of them. He went with them with his one boot and a slipper she had given him.

That young flyer, Harry J. Proskurniak, escaped the war and returned to Canada, but years later someone from Fjelstrup got in touch with him and found him happily married with two children. Although born and raised in Canada, his loyalty to the mother country, England, had inspired him to join the Royal Air Force. The mission on that fateful night took him over the southern part of Denmark en route to Berlin.

In memory of the other six men who lost their lives, a memorial was erected on the spot by the road where Vagn and Axel had seen the dead soldier. Two smaller stones give the names of the six men. A larger stone in the middle is inscribed with these words, translated from Danish:

Here fell
6 English flyers
d. 15.2.1944
They offered their lives,
We won our freedom.

At the end of summer on the farm we celebrated bringing in the last load of the harvest by decorating one sheaf with flowers from the garden and hoisting it up on a pitchfork. Everyone piled on top of the wagon and, typically Danish, we sang countless odes to our beloved land. A few weeks later a community harvest feast was held, and the farmers' wives skimmed a little cream from the milk to make illegal butter and whipped cream for the cakes. After the Germans issued a curfew forbidding us to travel the streets after 8:00 P.M., we did our celebrating in the afternoon, but we were giddy and carefree for that little while, singing and dancing for hours.

Those harvest summers were the last of my days as a schoolgirl. I became eighteen and had to think of a future and an education to prepare me to work. The prospects were slim in our present world.

Out of Limbo

My father spent more and more time fixated on the radio news beamed at us from London. A high-ranking politician, Christmas Møller, had fled to England by way of Sweden. Now we could hear him daily, even though sound-disturbance devices were used in an effort to drown him out. Only in this way were we tuned in to what was going on in the outside world. I clearly remember Father's anguish when he told us that Kaj Munk had been shot. Munk was a renowned pastor, philosopher, and poet. His daring, caustic sermons and bold poetry had inflamed the Nazis. On January 4, 1944, they took him out of his house; he was later found shot, lying in a ditch a few kilometers from Vederslev in Jutland, where he had lived with his family. Other Danish citizens disappeared in this way, too, but my father reacted to Kaj Munk's murder with especially profound grief and despair.

I was barely eighteen, and sick of the gloom. Willy had gone on to jobs away from our village. Gerda had started her training with a designer of women's clothing in Haderslev. Both seemed to slide into their professions out of necessity and opportunity, without much fanfare. Willy, small and slight, lacked physical strength, but he was a diligent worker and quite talented in business and in his chosen field of tailoring. I've wondered if Gerda went into that same field because of the severe eczema she developed on her hands, probably caused by our strong soap. It turned out that she did show a fine talent for design and construction of clothes.

I had no physical maladies. At 5'5", I was the tallest of the family, and was healthy and athletic. I wanted to enter nursing, but my choice of a career caused upheaval in the family. My father, otherwise loving and loyal, became an immovable object in his opposition. With the bleak outlook for his business, the store shelves empty, he would not commit himself to tuition payments for the several years nursing training would take.

Then my mother's sister, Aunt Ella, and her husband, Alfred, entered the picture, and communications totally broke down. They were a childless couple living about sixty miles west of Copenhagen in a town called Gevninge. I had spent many vacations with them as a child, and knew that they were quite fond of me. But when Alfred offered to open a bank account for me with two thousand kroner, with the agreement that I could pay it back without interest after my education was achieved, my good and proud father let Alfred know in no uncertain terms that his help was not needed. Adding to my woes was Mother's obsessive concern that I, like two retired nurses living in our town, would contract some horrible illness from a patient and live out my days as an invalid, as those two poor women had to do.

The controversy over my future shattered the peace of our home and put my future in limbo. My mother preached gloom and doom, and I retreated into long, lonely sessions of crying as I kept trying to mediate a breakthrough with either parent.

The solution came as a small ad in our newspaper. A student nurse was wanted in a children's home in the town of Gråsten, about forty kilometers south. The tuition was thirty-five kroner a month for a course lasting one year. With a flood of tears and much guilt-inducing cajoling, I finally got my parents to relent. I applied for the position, went on the train to interview, and was accepted.

For the white aprons I would be required to wear, Mother gave up some meters of the white sheeting she had hoarded for Gerda's or my trousseau. The blue uniform dresses she pieced together from pillowcases and tablecloths. I packed my little cardboard suitcase, ready for this next part of my life.

From January 1, 1944, through December 30 of that year, I learned to care for babies from birth through their second year. I studied anatomy, physiology, general health care, and the treatment of common childhood illnesses. I graduated with a certificate in pediatric nursing, such as it was. This training set the pattern for my life far into the future and in many ways affected the whole family.

I arrived in Gråsten on a cold January day. As it is in northern countries, there were few daylight hours, and the nights seemed especially long because of the curfew imposed on us by the German army. Together with other student nurses, I sneaked through the backyard over to the housekeeping school right next door. The children's home and the housekeeping school were closely associated. In return for their students having a chance to learn how to bathe and feed babies in our school, we received all our food from their experimental kitchens. We enjoyed many interesting and delicious meals, and their girls seemed to enjoy our babies. We also went to their school for handicraft lessons and gymnastics exercises, held on their large kitchen floor.

There were about twenty small children divided into three departments in the small institution called the *Gråsten Børnehjem* (children's home). Most of the babies arrived when they were four to five days old, from

Solveig with Eva (left) and Thomas.

Gråsten Børnehjem

hospitals or birth-clinics; most were later adopted. One little girl, Eva, had been taken from her home because of neglect and malnutrition, and she became my first primary care baby. She was about six weeks old. Her skin was covered with a severe rash, and the diaper area was raw and angry. She was so weak from malnutrition that she could make only weak squeaking sounds. In the months that it took me to nurse Eva back to health, I cleaned her skin with warm oil and applied wet sterile gauze pads to her raw bedsores. I held her and fed her every hour. I formed a total bond with that tiny child, despite the initial instruction I was given not to get attached to any of the babies.

I didn't know that during the months I spent nursing Eva, thousands of healthy babies, babies who had been loved and cared for by their mothers, were being taken to the gas chambers and ovens in the country just south of our border.

I had to part with Eva after about eight months. A young couple appeared one afternoon to pick her up. I had dressed her in a blue dress that I had made. It had white smocking on the chest. As I handed her to the beaming couple, her new parents, I learned the lesson not taught in our textbook—that love is to be given away, that it cannot be selfishly

Doing the laundry at Gråsten Børnehjem.

hoarded. Eva was mine for just a little while, but for that time I have remained grateful.

As the months passed and I studied and learned the routines, small babies came and went. If no home could be found, or if their parents were unable to care for them but didn't want to give them up, they stayed for a longer while. We didn't judge those parents, for we knew that the war had created all too many family crises.

Student nurses.

For us, too, the war made daily interruptions. Almost every night there were air raid sirens. At first blast we had to hurry into our uniforms and get the babies pulled away from the windows and outside walls. We had no basement in our old building, so we huddled in the hallways and against the inside walls.

After some hours we would hear the sounds of British aircraft returning from bombing missions, and then the all-clear siren sounded. On such nights, we got little sleep. Once order was restored and the babies were back in their rooms, we tumbled into our beds until morning shift started. But even as there were nights—and sometimes days—of fear, we also had times of fun and joy.

King Christian X riding through Copenhagen with a German plane overhead.

A Year in Gråsten

Gråsten is a small town with four to five thousand inhabitants. It is a lovely place, located directly on the Sønderborg Fjord. Surrounded by sea, forest, and parks, it is the home of the royal family's summer castle, a magnificent white structure surrounded with beautiful gardens. Crown Prince Frederick and his wife Crown Princess Ingrid and their three small daughters spent several summer months there. Unlike the British, the Danish royal family have always mingled with the population. We might meet Frederick biking with his daughters on the woodsy paths behind the castle, or see Ingrid shopping with them in the town stores. That the town was overrun by German soldiers did not seem to bother them. They just ignored the soldiers the way the rest of us did.

There was a large, fancy hotel by the fjord, cordoned off and occupied by soldiers. Many soldiers were stationed in Gråsten, probably because of it being a larger town with a harbor and a railroad. As I recall this, I find it remarkable that with all our disdain for these foreign soldiers, we had little fear of them. If we ignored them, they made no efforts to approach us, and they did not yell at us or try to get our attention the way young men will sometimes do. As it turned out, one of my fellow student nurses did make contact with some of them. Her name was Sonja.

Sonja was my first roommate, but I had been moved into another room by the time these events took place, and I had little social contact with her. I was shocked when she was called into the office of the head nurse and sent packing. Fraternizing with the enemy was an awful thing, and after the end of the war, girls who had been seen with soldiers had their heads shaved by the Danish underground forces. It must have been terribly humiliating to walk around afterwards with stocking caps covering their scalps.

We had one outlet for fun. On the outskirts of town there was an agricultural school with a student body of about sixty future farmers. To perk up their social life, they held dances once a month on Sunday afternoon from 3:00 to 7:30. Of course all of the housekeeping and nursing students were invited. There I met George, a very handsome twenty-four-year-old student from the island of Zealand. It is a terse understatement to say that I was swept off my feet. When he held me in his arms, I felt like Cinderella. As the winter months passed, I spent much of my spare time with him. We walked in the snow and spent hours in an old café on the main street, huddled in a dark corner drinking black rye coffee, sharing our secrets and dreams, for those few hours oblivious to the war's strife and gloom.

Alas, spring came, and George's schooling drew to a close. He had to return to his farm to get the fields prepared for seeding. I met him one day on the sidewalk right outside the children's home. He held both my hands. He had been looking for me, he said, to tell me his plan. He would go home, get his work done, and come back for me.

I was astounded. More accurately, I was scared out of my wits. I kept thinking, *Oh, no, George, this will never work.*

I didn't want to be a farmer's wife. I didn't want to cook and can and take care of chickens and slaughter pigs, year after year. "We'll see," I stammered. "We'll keep in touch." And we did write, but after a few letters, the romance faded into a sweet memory. I do still have his photograph in my album.

Summer came, and I was introduced to the Gråsten Rowing Club, and that took over my spare time. The clubhouse was within easy walking distance, and even though the German army occupied the upstairs, for some reason they allowed us to use the boats, downstairs shelter, and ramps. The equipment was old, but we had three sculling boats, each holding four crew members and a boatswain. With the moving seats and the long oars, these boats could move at a great, even speed. We also had a light one-man scull, very fragile and tricky to maneuver. Needless to say, none of us girls were ever allowed to use it!

There were strict rules for us. We could not go out more than 1.5 kilometers from shore. The boats had to be stored away by eight o'clock. But on Sunday mornings at six, we could sneak in the back door of the bakery and get rolls and bread and row over to a small island in the bay. There, a farm woman sold us illegal butter, gave us drinks, and we frolicked in the water and white sand for hours.

Rowing takes a lot of strength, but when my vacation time came, I was in good enough shape to sign on as a crew member for a trip around an island in the fjord. I borrowed a sleeping bag. The other three girls, Irma, her sister, Inge, and a small, tough girl called Marie brought the rest of the supplies. One brave fellow named Jack came along to man the compass. We slept in a tent on the beach and scrounged food from local farmers. We laughed and sang as we pulled those long, heavy oars day after day, and we made believe that the world was serene. The sun and salty water tanned us deeply, and my mother was dismayed to see that her daughter had turned a muscular brown.

With all our youth and energy, we felt strong, as if just being alive supported our beleaguered country. It was a horrible shock when one of our beloved club members was arrested and sent to Dachau, a concentration camp, where he died. We weren't told what he had done, and we were forbidden to discuss it, but we knew how much he hated the Nazis, and we assumed that he had been involved in the underground. We were told not to demonstrate in any manner, but we could not be stopped from crying for our gentle friend. We all put on our homemade white uniforms with the red insignia and went to church to pray for him.

Another death in 1944 was more public. It is written about in our history books. An army colonel in charge of the Danish border control, Oberst Swend-Paludan-Møller, had his home close to the castle in Gråsten.

During the night of May 25, the Gestapo came to arrest him. He sent his family to his neighbor Pastor Hvidt's house, and he waged a one-man war against the Nazis. Pastor Hvidt, bearing a white flag, tried to intervene, but the colonel was not persuaded. After he retreated to an attic room

Rowing.

and continued shooting, the Germans set his house on fire, and he died a hero, brave to the end. There were no sirens, but we heard the shooting. Because of the strict curfew, we didn't know what had happened until the next day.

We walked by his burned-out house. The news of the horrible event quickly spread over Gråsten, and thence, the country of Denmark.

The End of the Darkness

As 1944—and my year of training—grew to a close, the world seemed to have disintegrated into chaos. We knew that the invasion of Russia had failed, and we knew that the Allied forces had entered the war, but so successful was the German propaganda that we dared not underestimate their brutal force. As the Danish resistance movement escalated with growing success, the German troops retaliated with great viciousness, so we saw and heard the worst of them.

I focused on my work, studying hard and passing my November exams with good grades and a certificate. I was now qualified for positions involving the care of small children. Despite the upheaval and uncertainty of my country, I was preparing for a future.

I spent Christmas doing night duty. This was a two-week assignment for a shift from 8:00 P.M. to 7:00 A.M. My family and coworkers were sympathetic that it was my lot to spend the long, lonely nights of the holy

Oberst Svend Paludan-Møller died when the Germans burned his house. A memorial to him was built in Gråsten.

The castle in Gråsten.

season working. Gerda came down on the train on Christmas day. A young blond fellow, Nick Møller, who had stepped into George's place, was most solicitous, and his family invited both Gerda and me to dinner. I didn't lack for attention. Despite that, it was a sad, confusing time. I couldn't tell them that spending those two final weeks alone with the babies sleeping in their cribs seemed like the perfect touch. My deep sadness was not the result of missing Christmas festivities. It was because I realized that a very important chapter of my life was closing. I didn't want to leave the home, my friends, and the small children whom I had come to love so dearly.

In our torn-up world there was only uncertainty. Some years ago, I read a book entitled *So Many Partings*. I don't remember it very well, but the title has stayed with me as fitting for much of life.

The headmistress had put me in touch with a family in the town of Rungsted, on the island of Zealand. They had three small children and were looking for a nanny. After a few weeks visiting my parents, I found myself stuffed into a cramped train heading for Zealand. We needed a special pass to get onto the ferry that took us from Fyen to Zealand. The Gestapo searched our luggage as though we were traveling to a foreign country. Despite all their precautions, saboteurs were bombing the tracks almost daily.

We ended up sitting cramped together on the floors, in the hallways, and even in the toilets through the night. We were somewhere in the middle of Zealand, forbidden to leave the train. I hung onto my battered suitcase and waited with my fellow travelers.

At last we arrived at the Copenhagen station, but since curfew was still in effect, we could not leave until 5:30 A.M. I still had to take a train to Rungsted, about fifty miles to the north, and it was midmorning before I could call my new employer to say that I had arrived. Mr. Hartung told me where to go, and he walked to meet me and carry my suitcase. Like everyone else, he was without a car, so we trudged through the snow to his house.

After the uncomfortable long hours of my trip, I was sunk in such lonely sadness and total exhaustion that my memories of that first meeting are vague, almost dreamlike. Mrs. Hartung, a smiling young woman, greeted me along with her beautiful children, Pernille, Claus, and the baby, Ninette. They had moved into a country cottage owned by her father in order to get away from the dangerous Copenhagen streets.

Once again my youth and strength came to the rescue. I soon found my place in the family and took the children into my heart. A young girl did the cooking, so my sole responsibility was to look after the children.

Rungsted is located on the coast north of Copenhagen, a lovely small town. I didn't know then that it was also the home of the well-known author, Karen Blixen, of *Out of Africa* fame.

We were within walking distance of the beach. For the first time, I could see Sweden across the sound. After the almost total darkness of the past five years, I could hardly believe the sight of the whole coastline of that country lit up with thousands of lights. Again and again I returned and sat in the sand, gazing at the lights and trying to imagine our streets lit up, with bright lights shining from our windows. I was twenty years old. I had no way to know that in three months' time my dream would come true. Our lights would come back on, and the dark curtains would come down. The olive-clad soldiers would disappear from our streets and return to their broken land. On foot.

The war, at last, was over.

Solveig with Claus, Ninette, and Pernille Hartung

The Hartungs' house.

Five Long Years

Five long years of days passed by.
Spring came and went unseen.
But in the year of forty-five,
the fifth of May—The fifth of May
It all began to change.
Their war was lost.

The men in olive green
gave up their guns
and walked back south
to their ruined land.

Once again
our windows opened
Candles shone
In every sill.
We sang, we shouted,
we danced our way
back to our meeting hall.

FROM *MEMORIES OF THE GERMAN OCCUPATION OF DENMARK*
1940–1945
SOLVEIG SEDLET

Much has been written about the efforts the Danish made in rescuing their Jewish citizens. It was an all-out effort, and even though it was not known to most Danes at the time, it was amazingly successful. More than seven thousand persons were ferried across the sound to Sweden in the hulls of ordinary fishing boats right under the noses of the German patrol boats. Even though this has since been thoroughly documented in countless writings, most of us did not know about it at the time.

Living in South Jutland, I was not aware of one Dane being different from another. When I questioned my father, he assured me that in Denmark we were all Danes, none different from the rest. When rumors started circulating about the German concentration camps, I, in blithe innocence, did not believe that it concerned any of our friends or neighbors. I was, however, aware of the Danish resistance movement and that there were spies living secretly among us. I knew of the danger of getting caught, and I learned not to trust anyone outside of my family and closest friends.

Because our newspapers and radio broadcasts were controlled by the invaders, I learned nothing of the persecution of our Jewish citizens. I personally knew nothing about the horrors and the humiliations that they had to suffer. To this day, I find the thought horrifying and grievous. When asked, "Didn't you know any Danish Jews? Did you help any of them escape to Sweden?" I answer no, and people find it almost impossible to believe. But so it was. The Germans were able to hide their atrocities from us and rule our country with fear and secret brutality.

Ultimatum

This is an example of an ultimatum issued by the German government in August 1943. It was presented to the Danish King and his government, but was of course not found acceptable. (The ultimatum is not printed here in its full length.)

The Danish Government shall immediately declare martial law over the whole country. The martial law shall include following single measures:

1. It shall be forbidden for more than five persons to gather in a public place.

2. Any strike shall be forbidden as shall support for any strikers.

3. Any gathering in a closed room or out in the open shall be forbidden as shall travel in streets between 8:30 P.M. and 5:00 A.M. Restaurants shall close at 7:30 P.M. All weapons and explosives must be handed in before September 1, 1943.

4. It shall be forbidden to bother any Danish citizens who are sympathetic and helpful toward the German authorities or who have connection with the Germans.

5. Introduction of censoring of the news media under German guidance.

3

VENTURING AWAY

A New Life Away from Denmark

The Family Christensen: A Shaky Start

My first independent adventure was with a Danish family living in London, the Christensens. The only thing is, my sojourn with them did not begin in London. It began with an advertisement in the paper placed by Frantz Christensen, the father's father:

> Nanny wanted to care for two
> small children in larger home
> in London, England.

An address in Copenhagen followed. Near that ad was a similar one, for a position in Scotland, also listing a local contact.

I finished my studies, and then I worked in a day care center in Copenhagen. I went to the authorities for a passport. I had no plans in mind. Rather, I was waiting for something to happen. I was alert to possibilities—that was my strategy.

Then one day as I was polishing my shoes, working on a newspaper I had spread out on the carpet to protect it from stains, I noticed the listing in the classifieds.

It was as if a bell had sounded, or someone had called out my name. I finished the task at hand—the shoes, remember—and then I immediately sat down to compose letters in response to both ads.

I had developed qualifications, and I wrote out the details with a young person's confidence—I was twenty-one—and optimism. There was

109

my one-year degree in pediatric nursing; my position with the Hartung family in Rungsted; my present job at the day care center. I described these and offered to bring my recommendations with me to an interview. (Remember, there were no copy machines in those days.)

At the appointed time, I made my way to the address in Copenhagen where I would meet Mr. Christensen. The apartment was in an elegant large building in the very best of Copenhagen's neighborhoods. When I rang the doorbell, I was greeted by a uniformed maid who led me to a beautifully furnished sitting room. Soon Mr. Christensen and his wife appeared. They examined my credentials in a friendly manner, and the maid brought coffee on a tray with fine china and silver service. I did not know that Mr. Christensen owned a number of well-known ritzy restaurants and hotels in the city and also up the coast in the town of Fredensborg. Neither did I know that later on he would become an important factor in my life in other ways. What I did know was that he and his wife seemed to approve of me, and that I was able to chat with them comfortably.

They explained when the position would start and what the duties and salary would be. Their son, Vagn Christensen, was a branch manager for Scandinavian Airlines in London. The family lived in a rowhouse in West Kensington with their five-year-old son, Peter. The young mother was expecting another child in a few weeks.

I had also interviewed for the other position, in northern Scotland, where the family lived in an ancient castle and had horses I would be allowed to ride. London would be an entirely different experience in a great historic city where there were many cultural opportunities. I was offered both positions. I did not know either family, of course, and had no real basis for choosing between them except for where they lived. I did appreciate that the London family was Danish, so that my lack of English would not be a problem while I was learning it.

I chose London, but first I would meet the family at a summer cottage they had rented in the town of Gilleleje on the coast north of Copenhagen. I gave my notice at the day care center, worked the required final two weeks, packed my belongings, and got on the train for Gilleleje.

Mrs. Christensen was a tall, statuesque woman with flaming red hair. When she picked me up at the station, I saw that she was quite large with

Peter and Tove Christensen.

her pregnancy. I would be taking care of the baby soon, I guessed! Five-year-old Peter had come along, too, and we hit it off right away.

During the drive to the cottage, Mrs. Christensen told me she was tired of being pregnant, and was looking forward to getting it over with. She said she was very pleased that I had agreed to come. She mentioned that a visiting couple from London would be at the cottage, and she hoped that I wouldn't mind helping with supper. Later I found out that she came from a well-known family, famous for silversmithing and jewelry design. She had lived a pampered childhood surrounded by servants, with all the money she needed. During the war years, while Vagn Christensen served in the British Air Force, she had lived with her parents in Cophenhagen. Since that household had plenty of servants, she had not gained any experience in taking care of her son or in housekeeping. No wonder she was looking for help.

At the cottage she showed me to my room and went away to fix a tea tray for the two couples. She said she would leave cake for me and that I could fix my tea when I had unpacked at leisure.

In the kitchen, I found every counter covered with dirty dishes. Pots and pans crusted with last night's meal were stacked on the stove and in the sink. There would be no way to prepare tonight's supper with the kitchen in such a state. I changed clothes and started in on the dishes. There was only cold water, so I heated it, kettle after kettle. It took me hours, and all the while I could hear the two couples in the garden, having a great time. I managed to put away the pots and dishes, and I swept the floor. I never did have that tea.

The foursome made its way back into the house, and my, oh my, they were surprised to see the kitchen so clean. My mother had taught me well: "Don't wait to be told what to do," she would say. "If you see something needs to be done, do it." It was good advice for the work I had chosen. During the month we spent in that cottage, I had myself a job and a half while they looked for a maid. Since they were having no luck, I wrote a friend, Agnes Jørgensen, on behalf of the family, and for me, too. I didn't know her well, but I knew enough to trust she would be a good cook and helper. She accepted the offer, but it turned out to be quite some time before she joined us. By then we were in London, that location being the attraction for Agnes.

On the day the Missus decided to have the baby, she went to the hospital and had labor induced. The child weighed only five pounds, and I had deep misgivings about caring for her in an unheated summer cottage, but the parents wouldn't hear them. "You can do it, Solveig," they said enthusiastically. They bought space heaters for the nursery. When I bathed the tiny baby, everyone gathered around to watch in amazement. I never took a day off, fearing for little Anne Sofie. I did have time to walk along the beach in the evenings, and after a full day and my little outing, I was ready to turn in.

Happily, we moved from the cottage into a high-class hotel owned by the senior Mr. Christensen. It was called Store Kro, and was in Fredensborg. Suddenly, it seemed, I was in the lap of luxury, where every wish could be met quickly. I took my meals in the elegant dining room with Peter while Missus watched Anne Sofie. Then, while she dined, I walked with Peter and the baby in the gardens surrounding the Fredensborg Castle, situated just below the hotel. It was a lovely respite from the cottage, and I was much revived. A good thing it was, too, because I needed to be in shape for my near future and the next move.

The first six weeks in West Kensington turned out to be a repeat of the Gilleleje adventure. A sad, dusty rowhouse awaited us, and my working hours were long and tedious. What carried me through were the blessings of youthful energy and the gratitude of the Christensen couple.

The happy day finally came when Agnes arrived to take over the house and cooking chores and free me to focus on the children. She looked around and noticed how dusty the lampshades were! She would set the house to order, I could see. At last, things were looking up for me.

Upstairs, Downstairs on 68 Edith Road, W. 14 London

I was the youngest of three children in our family, and I had lived my whole childhood in a tiny village. My parents were understandably astonished when I called them from Copenhagen to say that I was taking a job in London, England. No one in our family had ever been away to a place so far, nor had anyone flown on an airplane.

When the day came for me to leave, my parents came across the country by train to see me off. I could see that Mother was upset, but Father's pride showed, mixed with a bit of envy of my ambition and courage. He had always been so interested in the outside world, had always encouraged us to read about it, yet he himself had never had the opportunity to venture out. World War I had robbed him of his youth. By the time it ended, he was already twenty-seven, and it was time to get married and take over the family business at the Fjelstrup Inn. He told me later that the United States had been encouraging young Scandinavians to immigrate and had offered them free passage. I never did confirm the details of this, but I felt the emotion that was a kind of loss when he told me that he would have gone to America if the times had been right. Sometimes it seems that that is one of the jobs of parenting: to make times right for our children to do what we never did.

In the excitement of anticipating my first ride in an airplane, I had not given the slightest thought to what it might actually entail. I was thinking of the glamour and adventure, anticipating the feeling of taking off into the air and leaving Danish shores behind. I would be waited on by pretty stewardesses, eating delicious meals.

Flying to England, 1946

Our plane had two engines. As one walked up the aisle, there was a hump crossing over the wheel casings. I was seated with the baby, Anne Sofie, in my lap as we taxied down the runway. I had not considered the turbulence over the North Sea, nor the possibility that I might get airsick.

I never did eat. I was much too miserable to take care of the baby or worry about anything except myself. Mrs. Christensen was sweet and helpful, and once we landed at Northholt Air Field, I soon recovered.

At the house, I settled in. Mrs. Christensen took me around to the registration offices where I got my rationing cards. Several weeks passed before I had a free day. I boarded a bus and rode into the center of London. Mrs. Christensen told me later that as she watched me go to the bus stop, she wondered if she would ever see this non-English-speaking country girl again. But I managed. It was heady stuff to walk the famous streets of London. I saw places I had read about, like Hyde Park Corner, Picadilly Circus, and Buckingham Palace. I felt like a butterfly emerging from its cocoon into a brand new world.

The Christensen home was a typical row house like thousands of others lining the streets of upper middle class neighborhoods in London. There were small differences from one street to the next, but the overall look was very much the same. The houses hugged winding streets for miles and miles. None were taller or fancier than the others, all being without grass, flowers, or other adornments on the outside. Each building was divided into four separate units along a narrow column, starting with the basement floor and going straight up for three more stories.

The house where I lived from 1946 to 1948 was in no way unusual. It was the third unit, and the only thing remarkable about it was that

68 Edith Road, 2004.

the fourth unit, having been hit by a bomb, was still a gutted-out ruin. Number 68 had survived. Four sturdy concrete steps led up to a portico with pillars flanking either side of the front door. One was well-protected there from the frequent rainy days. Each unit had a wrought iron lamp over the entrance door to guide visitors to the doorbell. The door was of dark stained oak, with a large frosted glass in the middle. It was so heavy, the bell could scarcely be heard from the outside.

Once indoors, one was greeted by a dreary dark red oriental carpet that ran down the front hall and up the staircase. To the right, a large double door led into two sitting rooms, each with a coal-burning fireplace. The front room had a bay window facing the street. With light-colored flowered coverings on the furniture and soft pastel walls and draperies, it was an attractive, cozy space. I later learned that the reason there were no plants or flowers in the room was that the fumes from burning coal would have killed them!

Another wide door led into the adjoining room, called the library. Furnished with a large brown leather sofa and deep, massive chairs, it was obviously a gentleman's room. The tables were stacked with periodicals and newspapers, but there were few books. A small balcony overlooked the boxy garden.

At the end of the entrance hallway was a cloakroom for guests and a water closet. The staircase led up to the master bath at the first landing. A large bathtub, as one still finds in very old homes, stood on legs. Most interestingly, the hot water heater was a large cylinder fastened to the wall between the tub and the washbasin. Copper tubing encircled the outside from the top to the bottom. Inside the hollow center of the cylinder was a gas pilot; when it was turned on, the water heated as it traveled through the tubing. A long spigot could be directed into either the basin or the bathtub to supply however much hot water was required. Although the contraption certainly was not decorative, I thought it quite ingenious.

Every morning, the upstairs maid drew a bath for the master of the house. He was very particular about the temperature, and she had to check it with a bath thermometer and get it just right before she went to his door to announce that his bath was ready. I didn't really know how seriously the master took this task until my sister came over and became the upstairs maid.

At about the same time, the cook, Agnes, would come up the stairs to knock on the master's door and ask what he wished to eat for breakfast. Unbeknownst to him or the Missus, all kinds of facial and other disrespectful gestures went on outside the doors in those hallways—our very own daily comedy act!

None of us were ever to address our employers in anything but the third person. "What would the master like for breakfast this morning?" Or, "Would the Missus be joining the children for tea?" This kind of formality is rather hard to grasp in this day and age, especially in the United States, where one is on a first-name basis with the minister and teacher. I was raised much differently, and old manners, drilled into my head from early childhood, are hard to let go. As children we had to curtsy even when greeted by uncles and aunts whom we did not see on a regular basis. It took me years not to rise when an older person entered the room, and it has been likewise difficult to accept calling an older person by first name, even when asked to do so. In my forties I was still curtsying when shaking hands with an important person! I was finally able to stop only because my children grew old enough to give me odd looks that made me self-conscious, but it was hard. Now that I am getting old myself, I sometimes wonder what it would feel like to enter a room and have all the youngsters stand up. There's a thought to ponder!

But let me return to Edith Road and the tall, narrow house. Traveling upward one more half-flight of stairs, one came to the bedrooms. To the immediate left was the master bedroom, nearly filled by a very large mahogany bed. All the bedrooms were heated by gas rather than coal. In one corner of the master bedroom, at a dressing table with fluffy gathered cloth trimming, I often helped the Missus arrange her hair before dinner. Both of us enjoyed chatting, and despite the formality, we were on very friendly terms. As the nanny, I spent a lot of time with her, and she liked sharing her thoughts about her life with me. She was quite an attractive woman, tall and regal. She kept her thick red hair quite long and liked to have it arranged in various, often exotic, styles. Her one problem was that she struggled with her weight—mostly, I thought, because she was so inactive. Sometimes she took me with her to Harrods when she shopped for an important outfit, and she learned to trust that I would recognize what looked best on her and would speak honestly.

A smaller bedroom and dressing room adjoined this room, and was sometimes used by the master. The Missus told me laughingly that he needed a night of rest every now and then. I gather she was a challenge to him, because he had a doctor come to the house to inject him with hormones on a weekly basis! They both also received the services of a masseur who came to the house once a week. In such a household, with three servants, nothing remains sacred. I would venture to bet that they knew far less about us and our private lives than we knew about theirs.

Further skyward, one came to the second landing bathroom, shared among the children and me. There was room enough for a good-sized table for me to use in dressing the baby, Anne Sofie, and later her little brother, Michael. It also served double duty as a feeding table and a place to work with six-year-old Peter on his homework. The same hot water gadget hung over the footed bathtub and sink, and there was a small rocking chair in the corner by the window. The gas fireplace kept the room cozily warm, and sometimes I felt sure it was the most popular room in the house. Both parents gathered there at times to gurgle at and jostle with their babies, a warm, happy family time that I enjoyed as much as they did.

Solveig and Sofie.

Peter's room was up the last half-flight of stairs, and beside it was a small one for me and one for the babies. Peter spent a lot of time in my room, seeking attention and reassurance, I think, to offset all the attention given to his siblings. When he was eight years old, he was sent away to boarding school. I well remember shedding tears as I sewed name tags into his clothes.

But there was another level in this house. All along I have described the Upstairs, but of course there was a Downstairs as well. At the end of the front hall, by the cloakroom, stairs led to a lower level. The dining room was quite elegantly appointed with dark oak furniture and chairs covered with heavy red fabric. On the other hand, the kitchen was surprisingly small. The cook and maid shared a sleeping room and bath nearby, and at the very end of the hall was the room where the big shiny pieces of coal could be poured in through an outside trapdoor.

The fireplaces were the only source of heat in these tall row houses, so each one had a row of six to eight chimneys on top of the roof, like you would see in the Mary Poppins movie. On foggy London days, the smoke from those thousands of chimneys made the air smell like smoked salami.

The maids could enter and leave the building through a downstairs door. There was also a small laundry room outside the back door, with an old-fashioned kettle where the clothes were boiled, scrubbed on washboards, and rinsed in large wooden tubs, then hung on lines strung across the small backyard. (No washing machines or dryers, of course.) A washerwoman came once a week to perform these cumbersome labors.

Sometimes I wondered how Agnes managed to prepare such good food in her dingy kitchen, but I never heard her complain. I took most of my meals with the children, except that I ate the evening dinner in the kitchen after the babies were put to bed. Peter ate that meal with his parents, something he sometimes seemed to endure more than enjoy.

Agnes, the girl who had come over from her family's farm in western Jutland, was a very good sport about the meager facilities, even though her own home was beautiful, large, and comfortable. Her cooking skills were impressive, too. When she arrived, I had already been in London for a few months and had picked up a bit of English, so it fell to me to do some of

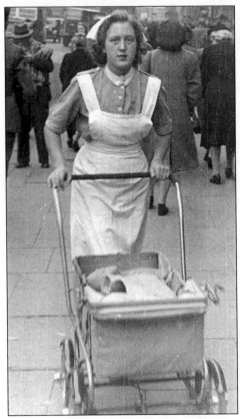

the shopping for her. This was not to say that I was an expert! I remember one day I tucked the baby in the pram and ventured to a nearby butcher shop. I had been instructed to buy a pork roast. To get ready, I consulted my trusty dictionary and looked up the words for *pig* and *meat*. I felt quite ready as I entered the store and spoke, haltingly, to the butcher. He repeated my

Solveig shopping with baby.

Gerda and Agnes in London.

request, and I could see that I had said something wrong. He couldn't keep a straight face as he turned to his colleague and sputtered, "This young lady wants some pig meat!" My face burned as it turned bright red, and his kind apologies made it even worse. From then on, every time I entered his store, he teased me, but I soon learned to laugh along with him.

The Upstairs Downstairs household, truly represented by that London one, is now a thing of the distant past. Imagine: a family of two healthy adults and three small children being served by three young adult women. Later in my life, I cooked, cleaned and cared for a family of six children in a ten-room house with no outside help. To add to that, I got involved in volunteer work for schools and the church, and with blood banks and civic groups. Thinking of that suburban lifestyle, and then the two years I spent in London, I can only say that being a nanny was like living in dreamland. Or better.

Springtime in London

The first winter in London passed quickly as I settled into my new life and routines. I went to classes at a school of language on Oxford Street. I learned to deal with the money system—twelve pence to the shilling—and I learned to get around on the buses and underground trains—the "tube." On my free evenings and the one day a week I had free, I spent hours at the nearby movie house, watching double features, sometimes twice. I carefully studied the mouth movements of the actors and learned new words and phrases. When spring arrived, I joined the Brits in celebrating the birth of a new beginning, a new year in which peace reigned over our world.

The scars of war were still evident all over London, even in the depths of the underground stations. The layered tunnels at Charing Cross and Victoria Street stations, to which only the year before thousands of citizens had fled during nightly bombing raids, still harbored the musty smell of the people who had camped next to the rumbling elevators. It was a sobering reminder.

Aboveground, the trees unfolded their leaves and the grass turned lush and green in Kensington Garden where I strolled with Anne Sofie tucked away in the pram. Princess Elizabeth had become engaged to the Greek Prince Philip (Elizabeth's third cousin—he shared with her a great-great grandmother—Queen Victoria) and there was much excitement building as their wedding approached. As in a fairy tale, the smiling twenty-year-old girl held the arm of the handsome blond prince. The timing could not have been better.

A small wedding was planned, in light of the economic stress of the time, but old customs prevailed in many ways. While I walked in the park I could see the royal guardsmen dressed in the full regalia used for royal celebration since ancient times. Wearing plumed hats and capes, and spurs, they practiced with the horses, getting them used to the crowds that would be lining the streets for the wedding. For the first time, I heard the wailing of bagpipes and saw Scots dressed in little skirts and tall furry headgear followed by marching bands with bugles and drums.

Legendary for their stiff upper lips, the British people are a resilient bunch, and their loyalty to the royal family never seemed to waver. During the terrors of war, the king and queen had stayed put in Buckingham Palace, luckily spared from bombs, while St. Paul's Cathedral, nearby, had gaping holes in its golden dome. I saw birds fly freely in and out while the sun shone onto the dusty pews. In the war's aftermath, London was dirty and grimy, the buildings blackened from soot and neglect. Still, it was clear that England would survive. Years later, after the buildings had been cleaned and repaired, I found the bland whiteness almost offensive.

Another fanciful reminder of love and romance was the great Royal Albert Hall, built by the young, grieving Queen Victoria in memory of her beloved husband, the father of their nine children. Widowed at age thirty-nine, she remained a widow for the rest of her life, and it was a long life. She died in 1901. I thought it romantic that in her sorrow she not only had the hall erected, but also had another memorial built directly across the street from it with a statue of Albert's likeness. In months to come, I often found my way to that hall for concerts, and to the British Museum located just behind it. I didn't need to know the language to appreciate music and art. Nor did I need English to attend ballets at the Covent Garden, where, to my delight, tea was served to us during intermission right in our seats by servant girls in caps and frilly aprons.

I had come in contact with another adventurous Danish girl named Gyda Uldall, an *au pair* with a family in Hempstead. With her I stomped the Hempstead Heath and visited the Kew Gardens. Together we sought out the newly formed International Groups. Gyda was not only unstoppable in her search for new experiences, she was also smart and great fun and tall and pretty in her own delicate way. Her English was better than mine, and without being brazen, she readily struck up conversations with some of the black men who had come in from the colonies. I had never seen a black person before and of course I was in total awe.

Gyda and I also explored the Indian restaurants of Soho, tasting spicy curried dishes and roaming the fascinating shops. It was all so different from little Denmark's homogeneity in population and culture that bordered on dullness. To our surprise we did run across a small Danish café in the labyrinth of narrow streets behind Picadilly Circus. We spotted the blue platters on the walls, and the red and white checkered tablecloths, and eagerly we ordered Danish meatballs and red cabbage from the menu. Just a little taste of home!

Together we shopped Oxford Street. I can still see Gyda modeling a bright red suit and a black bowler hat. With her narrow frame, straight yellow hair, and impish grin, she was stunning. When we entered the Hammersmith dancing hall, she attracted the attention of the low-keyed but marvelous dancers and she spun a yarn about her daring adventures, most of which she invented right on the spot.

"Don't tell them that you are a nanny," she told me. "Tell them you are working for the 'International Save a Child Organization.'"

It should not come as a surprise that Gyda later on became a well-known reporter for the *Berlingske Tidende*, Copenhagen's largest newspaper, and eventually she had her own weekly radio program, called *I Ro of Mag (In Peace and Leisure)*.

During her ambitious stay in London, Gyda developed lung problems that turned into tuberculosis, and she had to return to her home in Denmark. When I saw her there later, her father was sending her to Italy to get some sunshine. In her typical cheerful fashion she chirped, "Oh, well, I always wanted to go to Milano and open up a teahouse with rooms upstairs!" Wicked that girl was, but fun. I missed her terribly when she left.

But I am getting away from Kensington Park and the fanciful prancing horses. Elizabeth's wedding was to be small, but the energy and the exuberance of the people were hard to contain, and what could be a more appropriate event to celebrate than the union of a beaming young princess and her handsome prince? They were married on November 20, 1947. I had been in London a little over a year. We were glued to the radio. Television was still in its infancy, and the Christensen household did not have one. I did see a television set a few months later. Some people I was visiting invited me into a dark, smoke-filled room, where everyone was gathered around a small flickering screen. I thought it was a flash in the pan, and I lost interest quickly!

Over the radio we could hear the bells chiming and the soft voice of Elizabeth as she exchanged vows with Philip. We heard the blasting organ pipes as the couple emerged into the bright sunshine. England had come back to life, and continuity was established with the birth of their first son, Charles III, born a year later. It was a new spring, a new link in the chapter of history, and a remarkable time to be in England, for everyone, and certainly for me.

Even back in Denmark changes were taking place. The news reached us that our proud and beloved King Christian X had died, and his son, Crown Prince Frederick, whom I had seen bicycling with his young daughters in the park surrounding the summer castle in Gråsten, was crowned King Frederick IX on the evening of his father's death. A memorial service was held in a church in London, but the name of it escapes me. Dignitaries and British Royals gathered with plain folks like me to pay tribute to the proud man who had stood up to Nazi Germans during our five long years of occupation.

A Visit Home

After a year in England, the time came for me to make a trip home to Denmark. I packed my new clothes, bought at Selfridges's Department Store, along with gifts for my family. Although just about everything was strictly rationed in England, I had been pleasantly surprised to discover things we had not seen in Denmark for years. I can only suppose that the sad shape London was in after the relentless air attacks of the German Luftvaffe did not keep ships from bringing goods into harbor. Every two months, we were allowed ten small Cadbury chocolate bars—my favorites to this day—and one hundred cigarettes. Craven A and Players Cigarettes came in flat metal boxes holding fifty cigarettes in each. I'll never forget the excitement of opening that first box and seeing all those cigarettes lying neatly side by side, nor can I forget the sweet, pungent smell of real Virginia tobacco. Smoking was all the vogue in those days; we had not a thought about what it might do to our health.

After the war years in Denmark, when we subsisted on foul substitutes for coffee, tea, and tobacco, I loved the smell as much as the taste of the real things. I learned to drink fine tea, although I never learned to like it English style, with milk and sugar.

At home, we had been allowed only one quarter pound of sugar a month, and had become used to eating unsweetened foods and doing without cakes and cookies. It was therefore an out-of-this-world experience to go into Lyons Teahouse at Picadilly Circus and order delicious sweet

cakes with our tea. Bananas and oranges were a delight, too, but a rare one because they were so expensive.

As I looked forward to my trip home, I saved my rations of chocolate and cigarettes as gifts. I didn't think such precious wares could be safely carried in my battered, poorly-made suitcase, so I carried the goodies in a small cloth pouch. We did not yet have a term for "carry-ons" any more than we knew there would eventually be jet engines. We relied on two noisy propellers to carry us over the turbulent North Sea. Unable to fly at high altitudes, and buffeted by strong air currents, the plane bounced around mercilessly. I remember well my embarrassment at spending so much of the flight time with a paper bag in front of my face, the same kind of bag my children would call "urp-bags."

Once we landed, though, we moved slowly and there was time to recover. Checking passports, visas, and other papers was a long, cumbersome process, so very different from the efficiency with which hundreds of thousands of passengers spill out of huge planes today.

Once I was past the gate, I found Gerda waiting for me. Needless to say, by the time we left the airport, she was munching on a Cadbury bar and puffing one of those sweet-smelling cigarettes.

The plan was that I would stay with her a few days in the town of Tåstrup, outside Copenhagen, before taking the train to South Jutland to be with my parents. I was so excited about coming home, and I chattered on so about my happy times in London, that I did not notice Gerda's mood. Only when we were seated in her apartment did I see that she looked terribly sad, and that she had almost nothing to say. Then she started weeping, astounding me. I had always known her as my vivacious, outgoing sister. Not only was she popular among her friends, she was without a doubt the prettiest of all of us, with blond hair and bright blue eyes. Plenty of times I had looked at her and cursed my own mousy brown hair and ordinary gray eyes. I was the bookish one, hardly the thing to attract tall, handsome guys.

Yet here she was, tears running down her face.

"What in the world is the matter with you?" I asked her, totally bewildered. "Aren't you well?"

She sniffed and said, "I haven't been happy since you left. I never laugh anymore. I hate this boring town and boring job. I'm stuck, and here you are coming home to tell me about all the exciting things you've seen and done. Here I am, with nothing to look forward to." She was feeling very sorry for herself.

I could hardly believe my ears. She had always been involved in sports and recreational groups. She was always surrounded by great guys when I visited her. Despite all her social and athletic activities, however, she felt cheated, or perhaps she felt she was a failure, because she had never made a serious commitment to anyone or anything. Her big step away from home and her designing profession took her to a dry cleaning shop, as manager. She was floating along on a sea of boredom and loneliness when I appeared, bubbling over with enthusiasm. I assured her that she was a wonderful person, living a good life, but she could not be consoled, and, true to my nature, I set out to fix her up.

Stunned by her anguish, and passionate to make her happy, I managed, in a matter of a few minutes, to say, most unwittingly, the words that would put in motion a process of changing her life, and in the end, the life of my brother and my whole family.

"You can get a job in England, too," I reassured her. I added the ultimate promise: *"I will help you."*

I had not made such a promise to my brother, Willy, who had sailed his own boat away from safe family harbor. He should have done better, for all his defiance, because he had a talent that showed up in his apprenticeship as a tailor, and he passed his trade school courses with good grades and received a diploma. He even took advanced classes in cutting and designing. And he married a young girl, Grete.

Looking like a young man on the right road, he opened a small shop in an empty room in our parents' house, and the couple set up housekeeping in Grandmother Elise's house, in the upstairs apartment. His business grew enough that he took on an employee and moved to Christiansfeld, just seven kilometers (about five miles) away. From there, he moved to a larger shop and a larger house, gaining respect and acceptance in his community. He joined his father's prestigious club, the Odd Fellows. The couple adopted a little girl, Marianne. On the surface, his life looked good, but ever so slowly, small movements began to rock his boat.

In his larger house there was an extra apartment, and he rented the space to a couple with two small girls. The husband traveled around

Europe transporting merchandise, leaving his wife alone and bored. Her loneliness and my brother's boredom ignited an affair that broke apart two homes and left two small girls abandoned by their mother. Grete, the betrayed wife, packed up her child and belongings and went back to her parents' home on the Island of Sjœlland (Zealand). No one in the family ever saw her again.

The shame and disgrace and pain overshadowed us all. Our father, broken by sorrow, went away to rest in solitude, his dreams for his son, and for what they might have done together, forever gone.

Was it destiny or fate? Or was it simply character? God tests our strengths and weaknesses, and Willy did not pass the test. He was beguiled by a woman whose appeal was greater than his faith and his sense of responsibility. His life took a desperate turn as he felt the scorn of his community. In time, he, too, would turn to me. Although I would do what I could to help him, the repercussions of his bad choices would echo through his life.

Other Plans

I wanted to see the world. There was Paris, certainly, and on the other side of an ocean, the United States. Although I loved the children in my care, and I was happy that Gerda had joined me in London, I felt called to move on. The war had tied me down for five years without freedom under the German occupation, and then my training had had its discipline and routine, too. I had been in London for eighteen months, doing my job, studying hard to become fluent in English, and I felt ready to take on French. In Paris.

The elder Mr. Christensen, though, the gentle man who had hired me in Copenhagen, and whom I had come to know well from our family visits to his lovely summer home in Hornbœk, was not ready to see me go. He took me aside and offered me a grand incentive to stay six more months: the sizable bonus of five hundred Danish kroner.

Although I had planned to go next to Paris, I had also been offered a position in the United States, and had chosen that as my next move.

*Gerda and Solveig
in Paris.*

Considering Mr. Christensen's generous offer, I reasoned that there was more than one way to get to Paris.

With the kroner in hand, I grandly invited Gerda to a whirlwind tour of Paris. We booked a room in a pleasant, medium-priced hotel close to the center of the city. It was more than I could actually afford, but we saved by avoiding restaurants, eating salami, cheese, and bread in our room.

The harrowing trip across the Channel made both of us horribly seasick. We were convinced (and maybe hopeful!) that we would die quickly and escape our suffering. Once on solid ground, though, we quickly recovered. In fact, we ate salami sandwiches and got a good night's rest.

The next morning we set out, city map in hand, with a list of sights to see. Nothing went according to plan. First, I came down with a toothache for which aspirin did nothing. Then Gerda, who loved high-heeled shoes with ankle straps, all the rage at that time, got blisters that could only be soothed by bedroom slippers. Besides, rain poured down steadily. We spent precious money on a cheap umbrella for each of us, but in the end, alas, we spent our first day in the hotel, with stale salami and cheese and our pain.

The next day, things improved. The rain subsided, Gerda's blisters eased, and a druggist gave me something vile-tasting for my toothache. Things were looking up.

We headed for the Eiffel Tower, a choice that changed the direction of our so-far ill-fated trip. There we were, typical tourists, with maps and umbrellas giving us away. What true Parisian would be spending a gray, wet, ordinary Tuesday morning at the Eiffel Tower?

I don't know who spotted whom first, but soon we were in the company of two fine-looking tourists from Switzerland, Heinrich and Egon. They were handsome. They spoke French, German, and some English, and they were as short of funds as we were. It was a perfect match.

We spent the rest of the day sightseeing with them, and after a rest stop in our respective hotels, we arranged to meet at a corner for some night life. It was a good thing, too, because we walked in streets where girls should not go alone. We saw Gypsies dancing and swaying to the wailing sounds of the accordion. For the first time in my life I saw men dancing with men, explained in a whisper by my Swiss companion Heinrich as the behavior you find in a gay bar.

Later we stumbled into a small, quiet place with a two-piece dance band. We ordered two glasses each of champagne and brandy, mixed them together, and shared them. My Swiss knight pulled me to the dance floor. In that

Heinrich.

129

dimly lit club, accompanied by soft, sweet music, our two young, very tired bodies seemed to fuse into a single unit. Moving slowly, our arms entwined, we found comfort in shamelessly clinging to one another. It was, all at once, sensuous, romantic, and yet innocent, but best of all, and most accurately, we gave ourselves over to abandon. We knew we would never see one another again. We were two strangers in paradise.

I don't remember how Gerda and Egon spent their time in the café. Probably, Gerda's feet were not fit for much dancing. I do know that I wasn't the least bit concerned about what she was doing. My Heinrich and I had totally removed ourselves from being conscious of others.

We exchanged a few letters, and I was left with my memories and a photograph of him. There he is in my picture album, a handsome fellow standing with his skis on the slopes of the Swiss Alps. Ever so long a time after, he remains in my memory.

My last months of commitment to the London family passed. It was time to cross an ocean to another life.

— 4 —

TRANSATLANTIC

Coming to America

New Immigrants: November 1949

Gerda and I arrived in New York aboard the Swedish American Line, the SS Stockholm. Like so many thousands of immigrants before us, we stood at the ship's railing and watched the Statue of Liberty and the New York skyline coming into view. We knew we were facing many challenges, but we thrilled to them, because we did not face hardship, as others had.

Fortunately, I had a job as an *au pair* for a well-to-do middle-aged couple in New Jersey, John and Paula Slater. There were no babies to tend. The couple's three children were grown and married. My job was to help around the house. In return, I would receive a small wage and be allowed to go to school.

The SS Stockholm.

131

Gerda's decision to accompany me was a last-minute one. She had a boyfriend in Copenhagen, but the thought of me venturing to America without her was more than she could stand. She implored me to write Mr. Slater and ask if she could come along. He was such a good-natured, generous man, he agreed to sponsor her as well, so she put her boyfriend on hold and got ready to tag along. It wasn't an entirely easy decision, and at one point she begged me to advise her, but I drew the line at that. I felt secure about my own plans and goals, but I didn't want to make decisions for someone else, not even her. She was so uncertain, right up to the last moment, that Mr. Slater sent me a telegram on board the ship asking if she was with me or not.

John Elliot Slater was a powerful man, Chairman of the Board of a company called American Export Lines and of a Philadelphia engineering firm. Because he made the arrangements for our passage on the SS *Stockholm*, we received preferential treatment aboard. When we pulled into the harbor, he had us paged, and our customs and immigration formalities were expedited, putting us ahead of everyone else. Waiting for us dockside was his black Lincoln Town Car, driven by his private chauffeur. He had come to the harbor himself, to accompany us as we drove to New Jersey.

The luxury of our arrangements was only a part of our exhilaration on arrival. Certain moments occur in every person's life, times when a dream seems to be coming true, or the opposite, when things happen that become haunting memories. This time of passage, not just across the ocean, but into a new part of my life, held two such moments.

Forever etched into my soul is the sorrowful picture of our mother and father standing on the platform at the railroad station in Kolding, Denmark, as we prepared to depart. To this day I can see our mother reaching for the train as it began to move, as if she were trying to hold it back.

The other moment occurred as we were being driven out of the Holland Tunnel from New York. We passed through the dark, narrow tunnel and were spewed out on the other side, into the state of New Jersey, in a way that was like being born. I had the feeling of no return; my connection with Denmark was now forever severed.

Had I been by myself, I would not have been so burdened by guilt about leaving our mother, but I felt responsible for Gerda and guilty for not being strong enough to tell her that she belonged close to her family in Denmark. In time, she learned that on her own. After a year in the States, I was engaged to a wonderful man, Ray Hirsch, whom I had met shortly after I arrived. Our wedding took place on December 9, 1950, in Ray's hometown of Chicago. Mr. and Mrs. Slater traveled the long, tedious trip on the train, and Mr. Slater stood in my father's place to walk me up the aisle in the Nebo Lutheran Church. Gerda was at my wedding, but she felt abandoned by it. Lost by herself, she went home the following spring, her passage kindly arranged by Mr. Slater.

I thought it was the end of our lives together, and that I would no longer have to worry about her. I thought she would find contentment in a life that suited her, but in less than a year, she implored me to rescue her again. "Please help me come back," she wrote. "I cannot stay in Denmark. There is no place here for me anymore."

As before, I did help her. Ray and I took out a loan to pay for her ticket, and she came across the Atlantic by boat again. She was temporarily installed in our small apartment, sleeping on a cot in our living room. She began to look for a job. By that time I was working as an assistant to a dentist in Montclair, New Jersey, and as fate would have it, Ray was suddenly transferred to St. Louis, Missouri, so Gerda took over my position.

Again our roads split; again Gerda was left to her own devices. She rented a room and set about making her own life, one that eventually led her into an unhappy marriage and a move to Caracas, Venezuela. The move was to have lasted two years, but by now, it has stretched toward fifty.

Through the various phases of my life, I have learned not to rely on others to make me happy. I have also learned that I can't make others happy. I can try to do good things for people I love. I can lighten their burden. But it is not in my power to make someone happy. Gerda had a need to escape from something, and that something is still there. It has been her companion all her adult life.

※

But I have skipped ahead, and I want to tell about our home for a year with the Slaters. We took up residence in a secluded area called Essex Fells, on a hill surrounded by a woods. I appreciated the beauty, but felt the isolation.

The Slaters' Essex Fells house.

In Copenhagen and London, transportation had been easily available, but here we were cut off without a car. We were given a spacious room with a private bath and a breathtaking view, and the Slaters did their best to introduce us to other young people, but getting to and fro was difficult.

We had a lot to learn about the culture in this new country. We had never heard of Thanksgiving. We had never seen a twenty-five-pound turkey, much less cooked one. We had never seen sweet potatoes, creamed corn and onions, cranberries, and, worst of all, stuffing, crammed inside that ugly, cavernous bird.

Thanksgiving was a trauma for us. Suddenly the house was full of the Slater clan: the children, spouses, and grandchildren. There was a constant buzz as people sipped cocktails and talked and laughed happily. Meanwhile, I was put in charge of the turkey. I was reminded to baste it often, and after I had burned my fingers and arms on the oven racks a dozen times, tears streamed down my face. Every pot and pan was dirty, and it seemed I had burned myself on each and every one of them. Oh, how I wished to be back in London, pushing babies down Kensington High Street to the park, while Agnes, the cook, took care of the kitchen mess!

I don't know how that meal tasted, but it did eventually make it to the table. Mercifully, I did not know then that the whole performance would be repeated when Christmas came around. At least I was better prepared by then. Gerda stayed out of the kitchen, taking care of the tables and flowers. To this day she hates to cook and is a master at finding ways to avoid it. How I let her get away with it still baffles me.

Somehow, the holiday season passed. In January, Mr. Slater helped me to enroll in adult evening classes at the high school in nearby Montclair. I signed up for United States History and English. Gerda had the same opportunity, but she would not be persuaded to take advantage of it. Those first classes were the beginning for me of a pursuit of learning that continues right up to this day.

Mr. Slater was concerned that Gerda and I have an active social life with people our own age. In nearby Montclair, New Jersey, there was a residential YMCA where a good number of young professional men rented rooms. They held a social that featured a sing-along around the piano, and Mr. Slater arranged for us to go. Sweet fruit punch and cookies were served. The fellows were a nice group, among them one in particular, Ray Hirsch, whom I mentioned earlier. He was only one of many, all of them away from their families, and they were all immediately interested in the two young Danish maidens fresh off the boat.

After that introduction, we never again lacked for the company of young men. They were eager to show us around: we had our first pizza, our first banana split; we went to Radio City Music Hall to see the Rockettes. On Valentine's Day, another first for us, we received enough boxes of chocolates to open a candy store. Groups of us regularly gathered in a back room of a country inn, where we learned all the old popular songs, and we danced to the jukebox until closing time.

Mr. Slater played the part of father and protector. No young man took us out unless he passed Mr. Slater's scrutiny, including an invitation to the library for a bit of conversation. His kindness and unselfishness have been a guide to me all my life, and eventually I too extended hospitality to young people caught up in their first adventure abroad.

He left early in the morning to take the train to Hoboken, where he caught the Manhattan ferry. When I started taking classes in nearby Caldwell, he rushed home after work and ate a hurried dinner so that he could drive me the four miles—and after class he drove to Caldwell again to pick me up. Happily, as we went into the winter months, I had plenty of offers for rides home to Essex Fells, and Mr. Slater did not have to make that second run to Caldwell to meet me.

Though Gerda and I loved the attention we received, we also wanted to be independent, so we pooled our salaries to save for a car. We wore each other's clothes, except for shoes, since my feet were bigger. No one seemed to notice that we were switching dresses, although later some mentioned that they thought we had bought matching outfits. As our funds grew, we made contact with a Danish friend, Paul Wœver, who was interning at a Ford dealership in Hartford, Connecticut. He convinced us that he would get us the perfect car for the least money. He did get us a good car, but it wasn't cheap. And there were other concerns. We needed a license to drive. We had Danish licenses, but almost no experience, so we made arrangements with a driving school in Newark, New Jersey, signing up for a half hour each, saying it was all we could afford! I think the instructor was a bit fascinated by two young greenhorns wanting to learn to drive in American traffic—in half an hour! Things were more relaxed then, though, and we did learn quickly. We had to anticipate stoplights, for example, a handy skill. And he gave us a never-fail recipe for parallel parking: Look over your left shoulder as you turn your wheels. When you see the other car's headlights through your back side window, turn your wheel hard the other way. It worked then and it works now; I can fit a car into the tightest space. I don't recall looking at the clock, but I think our instructor did a good job and gave us a bit of a bargain.

We took the train to Connecticut, where Paul met us at the station in Hartford. He took us to the dealership and showed us our very first automobile, a 1936 Ford, a six-cylinder, stick shift, two-door model. Paul pointed out what good shape the car was in and said it had a newer engine. We were so happy, we managed to overlook its ugly olive green color, maybe because it was darker than the green of German uniforms.

We named the car Oliver, after the little green things in a jar used by Mr. Slater in his martinis. We paid $350. Today, that would amount to more than a thousand dollars, so it was a substantial investment. Paul and his wife put us up for the night, and in the early morning we headed south on the Merritt Parkway. True to Paul's description, the motor ran like a top, but he had not mentioned a small problem with the brakes.

Gerda and our car, Oliver

Cars then were outfitted with mechanical rather than hydraulic brakes, and they took some serious effort to control. My first indication that all was not well came at the first toll booth, when I was driving. I pushed the brakes with all my might—and proceeded to roll right by the booth. Gerda hopped out nonchalantly and gave the man his quarter, and I revived the skill our friendly instructor had emphasized back in Newark: anticipate stops well in advance.

Come to think of it, that is a useful lesson all the way around.

Traveling the Distance

I left New Jersey in a sick-green Ford V-8. It was 1950, only five years since the end of the war, and one could not be particular about such matters as the color of a car. Ray had reluctantly traded in his long, sleek blue Hudson with all its chrome and fins for the ugly duckling Ford. He didn't think the old Hudson was up to the distances we were to travel.

The distance for me was a lot more than miles to drive. For both of us, this was a brand new chapter in life. After dating for a year, we had decided to marry. He was thirty-one, I was twenty-four, and we wanted to settle down. Replacing his flashy Hudson with the staid four-door Ford sedan was a kind of symbol of stability for us. Still, I agonized a lot over that commitment. I knew that once I made those promises, I would not

Ray and Solveig become engaged.

return to Denmark and my family again.

We set the wedding day in early November, and Ray's stepmother, Olga, went about making arrangements in Chicago. She set up the church, the florist, photographer, and reception. I had only Gerda in this country—of course she would be my bridesmaid—so it was truly up to Olga to be family. And then, when all seemed to be in order, I ended up in the hospital with appendicitis.

Everyone had to be informed that the wedding was postponed to December 9, 1950. I had lost ten pounds and was lost in my fancy satin wedding gown. Olga changed the arrangements, none too happily, and Gerda nimbly altered the satin gown. Much later I would learn that Ray's family had begun to wonder about "that foreign girl" and just how stable she was.

As in fairy tales, there was a happy ending. Ray, Gerda, and I packed our suitcases into the Ford and began our drive. We got onto the Pennsylvania Turnpike, one of the forerunners of the superhighways of today. We passed through a number of tunnels now made obsolete by I-80. It was not Gerda's and my first experience with long-distance driving. We had taken our Oliver to Maine to the Slaters' summer home, and I thought I was familiar with the sizes of states, but Ohio was more than I expected. I thought it might never end.

*Ray and
the Ford.*

Frugal Ray had not bought the optional radio, and we were left to our own devices for entertainment. He had a terrific voice and an unending repertoire of old songs. He taught us many of them as the miles slipped by. We sang "Heart of my Heart," "By the Light of the Silvery Moon," "Daisy, Daisy," and many more, including the racy "Cigarettes and Whiskey and Wild Wild Women!" And of course I had learned many songs back in New Jersey on Saturday nights at the Wild Wood Inn, a place that was neither wild nor near the woods.

We had another source of entertainment in the car, given to us by Pastor Otheman Smith of the Congregational Church in Montclair, whom we

had come to love through his church group for young people. He was a kindly, fatherly man, and he had invited Ray and me to counseling sessions about the meaning of marriage. To reinforce his points, he sent us away with a how-to book. I'm

Traveling around the country, we stayed in the "motels" of the 1950s, which usually were groups of cabins.

139

The honour of your presence is requested
at the marriage of
Miss Solveig Elise Petersen
and
Mr. Raymond Charles Hirsch
on Sunday, the nineteenth of November
at three-thirty in the afternoon
Nebo Lutheran Church
North Menard Avenue and
West Dakin Street
Chicago, Illinois

Owing to the illness of
Miss Solveig Elise Petersen
her marriage to
Mr. Raymond Charles Hirsch
has been postponed until
Saturday, the ninth of December
at four in the afternoon

The wedding had to be postponed when Solveig ended up in the hospital with appendicitis.

sure it was packed with good advice, but now, more than fifty years later, the only thing that comes to mind is the admonition that continued bliss in the marriage bed comes through the shower, and should be fortified with liberal applications of Sweetheart Soap! All I remember about the rest of the book and its no-doubt sensible tips was that we kept breaking into fits of giggles and belly laughs, not quite the reaction the good pastor had in mind.

I regret that I lost that book. It would have caused great mirth among my children, and my grandchildren, too, as they approached the marrying age. Who knows? Perhaps it would have given them some fine ideas; all they would have had to do was switch from Sweetheart Soap to something like Dial!

On our wedding day, it snowed and then froze, covering the ground with ice. If it had not been for the many strong hands helping me, I surely would have slid down the church steps with my long train behind me and those new satin sandals on my feet. On that day, turmoil, unbelievable happiness, and the sense of an enormous commitment all mixed together: this was to be a life so far from my parents, truly an end to all that had been my childhood. Mother had sent sprigs of the myrtle plant taken from the one she had nurtured on her windowsill for many years in anticipation of her daughters' marriages. In Denmark the custom is to make a wreath from the myrtle sprigs and use it as a crown to hold the bridal veil. As a symbol of the mother's love, it bestows blessings on the marriage and the children of the union. Of course Gerda and I were thinking of this as she helped me fasten the sprigs on my veil, and neither of us could speak.

I still have that gown of heavy satin with its long train, now yellowed with age. The red roses Ray gave me to hold, and the myrtle, have long since crumbled away, but the dress has withstood many moves. At one time it was stored in a little room under the basement steps, and there my children's

Gerda helps Solveig dress for the wedding. Note the myrtle sprigs in her headpiece.

Mr. Slater walked Solveig down the aisle.

hamsters built a nest in it. If the myrtle twigs were supposed to signify fertility, it seemed to have served the purpose, as the hamster family had ten lively babies! Still, the dress survived its temporary use as a maternity ward.

Ray had, true to his nature, studiously and carefully planned our honeymoon in Williamsburg, Virginia. He figured that Virginia, being farther south than New Jersey, would also be warmer, but he had not reckoned on the particularly severe winter of 1950. We drove south through Kentucky, Tennessee, the Carolinas, but found no relief. The roads were icy and we saw semi-trucks jackknifed along the way. So it was that we ended up in Florida, with its wonderful warm, sunny breezes blowing in off miles of white sandy beaches. The palm trees and orange trees lining the roads seemed to be welcoming us to paradise. Weary though we were, we quickly found a cabin, pulled out our swimsuits, and headed for the beach. We didn't worry about harmful rays or sunscreen; we baked, and it was wonderful.

We had three days left before Ray had to return to his office. Lying in the sand, one of my brilliant ideas popped into my head. "Ray, Ray, wake up," I said, barely giving him time to do so. "I've got a great idea. Why don't you fly back to New Jersey, and I'll drive the car back by myself. That way, we'll have three more days in this wonderland." Even my sensible husband thought this reasonable. We splurged on champagne with our dinner to celebrate our extra days of freedom.

Ray and Solveig cut the cake.

Nonetheless, our honeymoon came to an end. I dropped Ray at the St. Petersburg airport and steered the car north on Route 1. Reality hit me. It is a long, long way from St. Petersburg, Florida, to Montclair, New Jersey. It occurred to me that if I had driven twelve hundred miles in any direction from Denmark, I'd have ended up in the middle of the Sahara or on the bottom of the ocean. Yet here I was, taking off on my own. Route 1 was mostly a two-lane road, and as I drove through the southern states I was horrified to see signs posted that said, FOR WHITES ONLY. I had read history about the freeing of the slaves and the Civil War, but those signs made it suddenly real. I saw the cotton fields I had read about in *Gone With the Wind*. There were even signs warning of wild pigs. I ate southern-fried chicken and catfish, and with breakfast, grits. I slept in little cabins that looked like slightly enlarged beehives. You found them all along the way, replaced now, of course, by fancy motels.

At night I called Ray to tell him where I was. He said that the people in his office gave him a good razzing when they learned that his new bride was not at home waiting for him with a scrumptious dinner, that she was still on her way home from the honeymoon! "Are you crazy?" they needled him. "You let that girl, just over on the boat a year ago, drive away with your new car, your money, and your wedding gifts? You'll surely never see her again!"

But I reached Baltimore and its miles and miles of row houses on the third day, driving in rain. I was tired and sore from sitting, and when I pulled in at a truck stop that had cabins for rent, a kind lady put me up in her own house and fed me dinner. She obviously did not feel I was safe out there with rough and tumble truck drivers. The next day I was back on the road, more familiar now with the new country that was to be my home for the rest of my life.

I had traveled alone, and as it turned out, after only thirteen good years and four children, I traveled alone once again. My beloved husband Ray died at the age of forty-five after a cerebral hemorrhage, and I would have to call on my resources in a way I had never imagined.

Ray was buried the ninth of December, 1963, on the thirteenth anniversary of our wedding, next to his family at Mt. Olive Cemetery. Like our wedding day, it was a blustery cold Chicago day, but this time it seemed no better day or weather could have been possible.

Ray Hirsch
July 11, 1918 – December 5, 1963

WIDOWHOOD

A Year in Denmark

December 5, 1963

It was a cold December morning like any other. Three little girls dressing for the day, breakfast on the table. Changing the baby's diaper, I looked at his face and I thought: You have eyes just like your father.

Ray was in the bathroom, his face lathered with shaving cream. I put my arms around him and laid my cheek against his back.

"I love you," I said. "I'm glad you came home safe from your trip yesterday."

I left him to his scraping, but I saw his eyes in the mirror; I saw the smile for me that was there.

You wonder why a terrible thing happens, if you did something to deserve it. I didn't forget to be grateful. I knew how lucky I was. There was the sweet smell of this small boy, John, born six years after the last girl. The burble of the coffee pot. My husband kissing his

Our house in Downers Grove.

Karen, Solveig,
John, Ellen,
Ray, Nina

children, and me, goodbye for the day. The chatter of our daughters as they got ready for school. I remember I decided to make a cake for Karen's birthday—a little late, so that we could celebrate with Daddy home. I knew how fortunate I was, to make a home for our beautiful children, to depend on a husband who loved us all, a man who worked hard to provide.

Then the phone rang. I held the baby in my arms. I looked at the clock: not yet ten.

"Mrs. Hirsch?" Someone spoke kindly, someone I did not know. "Your husband has been in an accident. We think you should come to the hospital right away."

I had to lay the baby down so that I could write directions. We had moved recently to this town and I didn't know my way. I made the notes, and then I asked, "Is he going to be all right?"

I heard, "We're doing our best," and I knew nothing would ever be the same.

A neighbor came to take care of the baby. Another neighbor, Mrs. Dicke, drove me to the hospital. She was an older woman, a little nervous.

146

She took a wrong turn and had to ask a mailman the way. I could have said, *Don't worry so, there's no need to hurry.*

※

A nurse took my hand. As soon as she spoke, I recognized her voice from the phone call. She couldn't say the word dead; instead she said, "Your husband has deceased."

All sound stopped. Everything silent, still. "Take me to him," I said.

One of his shoes had come off. *Sorry, sorry,* everyone said. No one likes to give the worst news. Someone gave me the odds and ends that had been in his pockets.

"Your brother has died," I had to say to Ray's only sister, Carol, in Indiana. *Sorry.* The two stepsisters, Loraine and Dorothy, in Chicago. *Sorry.* And then my brother, Willy, in St. Louis. *Call Gerda in Venezuela.*

Sorry, I said to Carol, telling her that I couldn't be the one to call his parents. I couldn't bear the thought of his father's voice when he heard his only son was dead.

I sent a telegram to my parents' friend, a minister in Fjelstrup, Denmark, where they still lived.

Then I got ready to face my daughters.

※

Three little girls came bursting through the door, as children will, breathless from running, their cheeks red from the crisp winter air. "Mom, Mom," they called out, "Is Dad all right? Where is he?" They had been told there was an accident, with his car; just an accident.

I met them in the front hall. "Come," I said, "Let's go upstairs, I have to tell you about Daddy." Those three pairs of eyes were searching my face.

"Your daddy was so badly hurt," I told them, "that he could not live, and God is caring for him now. He is in good hands, and we will have to live without him."

How could my children understand death? I thought. They were only six, eight, and ten years old. They had no experience with people dying. I needed to tell them that their father's spirit would always be with us, that only his flesh was dead, not his soul and spirit.

"We will miss him," I said to the crying little girls, "but you will see, he will be part of us all the rest of our lives. He planned and cared for us. We will be all right. His love for us was special, and we will have to stick

This studio picture of Ellen, John, Karen, and Nina arrived after Ray's death.

together and help each other, and you will see, we will be all right and make him proud."

They knew they could trust me and their dependable father. They looked at my face and eyes, and they knew things would never be the same, but we had each other, and we had our baby, John.

It was such a small thing, a tiny blood vessel that burst open and flooded his brain. His car careened out of control on the superhighway until it was halted by a solid cement abutment. Whether he died from that impact or from the rupture in his brain we could not know. We knew only that it was quick, brutal, final.

The house filled with food and flowers and loving, caring people. Pastor Cook, from the church we had joined only a few months earlier, who had welcomed our baby into the church family in the presence of the grandparents visiting from Florida, now spoke to his congregation and urged them to reach out and help this young mother and her four young children. The women barely knew me, but they gathered in my kitchen ready to serve food and love. The assistant pastor, Rollin Johnson, had come as soon as the news reached him, and he faithfully stood by my side. He helped me through the decisions that had to be made—which funeral home, what flowers, songs to be sung, clothes to wear.

I walked around quietly, shielded in my black clothes. I fixed my hair and bought warm knitted hats for my three girls, and we brought my husband, my children's father, to the Mt. Olive cemetery on the ninth day of December, a bitterly cold day in Chicago. Back at the house, I floated through the day, wearing black, doing what had to be done. When my friends cried, I was the one offering reassurances: *We'll be all right. I'll call you if I need you.*

That night I took the baby to the warm kitchen for his bottle. In the dark window glass across from me I saw myself, a young mother feeding her infant. It was the same girl who had ventured out into the world with a head full of dreams and adventure, and now she was a mother alone with four children. There was no family near now. I faced a new challenge: I had to bring up my children alone. But of course God was there, and I was not alone.

When Christmas came we boarded a train in Chicago and went to Indiana, to Ray's sister Carol, her husband, Ed, and their three children. Carol and I cooked and baked, shopped and cleaned. We decorated the tree and the house, inside and out. Our seven children would have a happy Christmas and we would put our sorrow away for that little time.

When their Uncle Ed was home he played with all the children, and he rocked the baby through the football games on TV. We stayed through the holidays, until it was time to return to school, and then we went home on the train.

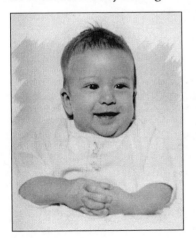

The house settled into a soft rhythm. Days passed quietly like whispers, into night, and day again. The children came and went and the baby sang his little songs of need—to be held, fed, hugged,

John at three months

kissed. The girls watched. For there is this with children: They need things. They need routine, and songs, baths and meals. They need for their mother to put their lives back together.

Through those winter months, I stayed inside, wearing black, a measure of security, or perhaps I was clinging to the old customs of my childhood home.

And then one day it seemed that winter had lost its grip. The sun warmed us. My sister arrived with her two children, Paul and Charlotte. Coming from Venezuela, they had no warm clothes for winter, so we shopped and shared, and all the cousins played and laughed. We packed them into beds at night and then she and I huddled as we had as small girls back in the Fjelstrup Inn. We comforted one another, and I began to make new plans.

"I have to sell this house," I told Gerda. Everyday problems had crowded in on me throughout the winter: the furnace, the sump pump, accidents and illness.

When the furnace quit, help came through a solicitous telephone operator who, in the middle of the night, helped me find a repairman on twenty-four-hour duty. After he came and scooped buckets of soot out of the clogged chimney, he asked about my husband. "Where is he, anyway?" he said gruffly, seeing me there with my bundled baby in my arms. When, reluctantly, I told him that my husband had died only weeks before, he broke into tears. "I'm so sorry," he choked. "I never should have asked. I'm so very sorry."

Fortunately the kitchen had a gas stove and there I could keep my children warm when we woke up in the morning. So upset was that poor, gentle repairman, he would not let me pay him, and in the weeks that followed, he called to check on us, to be sure that we were all right and that the furnace was working. A few weeks later, the sump pump gave out and the basement flooded, and it was just after Gerda arrived that the washing machine quit. Someone ran into my VW bus with six kids and Gerda in it with me. And then I caught the mumps from my middle girl, Ellen.

The fever was barely gone and my face was pale and still misshapen when I went to see my lawyer, Alan Hultman. By now he was my trusted friend, and wise enough not to offer too much sympathy as I told him of my calamities.

"Life goes on," he said quietly. "Like a train in motion, there is no time to get off."

I had taken my father-in-law aside at the grave and told him that I was going to take the children to Denmark for a year. I knew I would have to get ready, it would take a lot of planning, but there comes a time when even a mother needs her own mother and father.

Before Gerda went back to Venezuela, I was able to sell our big house (so recently bought!), and I bought a smaller one a few blocks away. Neighbors helped me move, and I painted the rooms. With spring's warmer days arriving, I finally shed my black clothes and put them away in the back of a closet. It was the right thing, to begin in a new place, to make a new home, the five of us. The girls were in school and the baby, John, was waking up to the world and the rough and tumble boys on our street. The future became prominent over the past, but the memories were a part of my life and would sustain and comfort me during the years to come. Now, though, I moved forward into a new part of my life.

I moved toward my goal. We spent our second Christmas at Carol's house in Indiana, our second Christmas without a father. I bought tickets to

Our small house in Downers Grove.

Europe and made arrangements to pick up a Volkswagen bus in Frankfurt. I knew I would want to show the children all that I could, so I ordered it to be equipped with a table and benches and a small refrigerator. We would sleep and eat in it.

I rented our house to a nice couple and arranged for my lawyer to collect the rent and keep track of things for me. I spoke to the principal of my daughters' school and went away reassured that the experience would more than satisfy their educational requirements for the year. Indeed, he said he would like to go with us!

We took our clothes and our passports and walked out of the house. I felt that my renters were good people who would take care of my things, but what did it matter? *Things* did not seem very important any more.

A friend drove us to the airport.

I was on my way to my beloved parents.

Going Home

How often I had told my husband, "We'll go to Denmark, all of us. I'll show you where I grew up." We were in no hurry. The children would get more out of it when they were older, we said. We would pay off the car. We would get a house. Save money. The future, for a young family, stretched before us.

Now the future was here, and I alone was on my way to Denmark with our children. Two of the girls, Ellen and Nina, age ten and eight, were stretched out on the aisle floor of the plane covered with a pile of blankets brought by the attendants. Baby John, barely twenty months old, lay nestled in the covers too. Karen, who was twelve, was awake, resting on the empty seats. It was dark and quiet; most passengers were sleeping.

Through the long night, I ached for my beloved, gentle husband. I longed to hear his voice, to feel his hand on mine. I realized that this trip was a pilgrimage for us, a way to honor him by fulfilling a dream we had shared.

Beside me, Karen whispered, "Are you all right, Mom?" She had grown up fast, though she was so young. She helped me with her siblings, so dependable, so responsible, worrying for them, and for me. During the long winter she had sometimes asked me, "Are you lonely when you go to bed?" Or she would say how glad she was to hear me play the piano or talk on the phone—so that I wouldn't be lonely.

I told her I was fine, but neither of us could sleep. I was so grateful to arrive in Copenhagen, to board the shuttle to South Jutland, to pass through the gate into the arms of my parents and their friends, Johanne and Laurits Larsen. We cried, but there was much to do with the children and the bags. Then we were driving. All of us were silenced by our emotions on the drive. It was enough to look out on the gently rolling Danish landscape, so fresh and green in the spring sunshine.

At home my mother and Johanne fussed over the children. They fed them and showed them to their beds in the upstairs room. I went up to kneel and hear their prayers, and then we tucked them in with hot water bottles under the down comforters, just as Mother had once tucked me in.

When I went up to join the children, I climbed into the small bed in the corner of the room. My grandfather Søren Wilhelm Petersen had built it with his own hands when he brought his young bride Elise to the small town of Fjelstrup. It was now painted green, and it was too short for me. The mattress was hard and lumpy, but as I tucked the old feather quilt around myself, a strong feeling of safety and peace settled over me. I was home and safe. My mother and father were right downstairs visiting with the Larsens, just like times long past.

Our life in Denmark had begun. I knew my instinct had been right, that we would heal here.

※

After three days of relaxing and unpacking, it was time to get the VW bus I had ordered in Germany. We needed it in order to be independent. Reluctantly, I left my children with their non-English-speaking grandparents. Karen took over the mother role and with no common language except the language of love, they all managed while I made my way back to the airport and from there to Frankfurt. A bus took me into the city and I found my way to the offices designated for my pickup.

A surly, chubby, bespectacled man met me at the reception desk. His mustache was neatly trimmed. He wore a gold watch in his vest pocket and a heavy gold chain draped across his ample stomach. A sign on his desk said *Herman Krause, Direktor.*

I handed him my papers and told him why I was there, and he disappeared into an inner office. I sensed trouble. The long occupation during the war had made me wary and distrustful of Germans. I admonished myself: *The war is over, they aren't all bad, calm yourself.* Still, I wondered.

After some time Mr. Krause returned with my papers in hand and said that everything was in good order. "You can pick up your car in the morning at nine. Come back to this office then," he said in his strong German accent. He was talking down to me, he was a pompous man, and I felt anger building in me. Inside me, a little voice warned me not to lose control, but I could not be restrained by that. Tired, sad, and terribly lonely, I broke out in a tirade of fury and frustration. It was not like me, but once I began I could not stop.

"This will not do!" I panted. "I need my car today, and you shall give me my car today or you can keep it forever!" The words tumbled out. I was screeching at him and smashing my fist against the counter where my papers lay.

I could hear myself growing shrill with rage while hot, angry tears streamed down my face. I hardly recognized myself. I was frustrated, true, but I was also humiliated and angry from the German occupation, and this was the first time I had had an opportunity to let it out.

Portly Mr. Krause tried to subdue me as he might a naughty child. "How do you expect me to get you to the car lot?" he huffed. "It's three o'clock in the afternoon, and the lot is out of town."

Once I had bent to Germans dictating my every move, but now I had a right to my car. I had paid for it, it was mine, and I wanted it *right now.*

"You are going to take me," I said. "In a taxi if necessary." I was sputtering. For extra emphasis I yelled, "NOW!"

Amazingly, I shortly found myself in a taxi. Krause came along, but he distanced himself by sitting with the driver. Soon enough we arrived at a huge car lot and swung up to a small building. Krause went inside with my papers and returned with the keeper of the lot. They had a bit of conversation, Krause adding a lot of gestures. Even at a distance I understood the gist of it: *We have this hysterical American woman who insists on getting her car today. Be careful with her, for she has a rotten temper.*

He glanced at me with disgust as he turned my papers over to the lot man, one Mr. Kurt Steinhoff. Krause hopped in the waiting taxi and left.

Mr. Steinhoff addressed me calmly. "You do not look too fierce to me."

I told him that I was Danish American and that I had understood quite well what Krause said about me. Mr. Steinhoff gave me a cup of coffee and a place to sit, on a bench, while he went for the car. I had ordered a cheery red color, but when he came driving up with an ugly light gray one, I was too spent to protest. I was more concerned about driving with a four-gear stick shift 350 miles to Denmark.

"You'll be fine," he said. "I'll take you on a trial run around the lot."

I had worn a royal blue suit with a short skirt, and getting up into the bus was most awkward, but I had no choice. I hiked up my skirt, got into the driver's seat, did my turn with Mr. Steinhoff, and then made my way to the famous German racetrack, the Autobahn.

On an American highway, I might not have thought so much of a 350-mile drive, but the German Autobahn is quite a different matter. As I eased onto it, I was immediately greeted with a loud honking from a trailer truck infuriated by my cautious entry. This was my first lesson.

Soon I fell in with the traffic and drove north until dark. Near the town of Kassell I spotted a sign with the familiar word MOTEL flashing. I parked and entered what looked like a converted castle.

Within an hour I had eaten, showered, and passed into a state beyond sleep. There was no space in my overloaded brain for sadness or worry. Deep, merciful sleep drowned out everything.

At daybreak I dressed quickly in my same blue suit. No one was at the counter, so I left the money with a note and stepped out into the cool morning air.

Back on the Autobahn, I did all right as early morning drivers whizzed by me. But rain began to beat on my windows, and after a while, the wipers quit working. I had to slow down. Impatient drivers flashed their lights at me. Their wheels sprayed me as they passed. I could hardly see. Fearfully I watched for an off-road parking place, and when I spied one, I quickly pulled off and just sat there. The strength I'd shown in my battle with Mr.

Krause was long gone. Here, I was simply an extremely sad woman sitting all alone in the middle of Germany longing for her children and her dead husband. I couldn't cry. I could only moan.

The rain thundered down on the metal roof and blinded me. Then someone covered in a military poncho was at my window, knocking. Guardedly, I rolled down the window. A man with a deep southern American voice (Arkansas, as it turned out) said, "Hi there, you having some kind of problem?" If he had come from outer space I could not have been more surprised. Or relieved.

I stammered out the tale of my broken wipers and the rude drivers and the rain. "Don't you worry," Arkansas said. "Give me your tools and I'll fix it for you."

He was young and tall, with wet reddish blond hair. He gave me a grin and an A-OK sign. After his final trip to his own car, he returned with a bag of cookies and a thermos filled with coffee. He climbed onto the seat beside me.

He said that he was with the U.S. military police and that he was on his way to Bremerhafen to ship his own car back to the States. His duties were nearly over. He had noticed my international license plate and rightly guessed that I was American. For one thing, he said, I didn't drive like a German. At that, both of us grinned. Then we sipped coffee and I told him a little of my story. I could feel tears burning behind my eyes, and quickly I shifted the mood by thanking him. "Next time, though," I said, "leave the sugar and cream out of the coffee."

His laugh broke the tension and we chatted a while. We decided we would drive somewhere and have lunch before our roads split. We settled on a small town just south of Hamburg, and he promised to follow me and keep a watch.

True to his word, he did so. When I had to stop for gas and thought I had lost him, I found him waiting up the road. Soon we found the roadside eating place, arriving in tandem.

After we ate we joked about the endless varieties of German sausages, and I had my black coffee. We said our good-byes in the parking lot, and just before he helped me climb into my car, he impulsively hugged me and wished me good luck. For that moment I loved him, just for being there. Such a casual meeting, a matter of accident, and yet it stays with me even now. Arkansas came just when I needed him, reminding me that there is good in one's fellow humans. For years I kept his address but I never wrote him, not even a thank you. I thought of him, though.

The last hundred miles were tedious, but as I drove up the hill toward Fjelstrup and spied the familiar church tower, I felt alive again. Everyone was waiting for me in the driveway as I drove in. My children wrapped their arms around me. I knew that wherever we were together, the five of us, we were home.

A Grand Occasion

Mother had urged us to come in time for the twenty-fifth wedding anniversary of Uncle Thomas and Aunt Kirstine. She was most insistent, so though it meant taking the girls out of school a little early, I adjusted our departure date. After I thought about it a while, I realized that what my mother really wanted was the opportunity to show off her grandchildren. After all, her children had all settled far away, Willy in St. Louis, Missouri, and Gerda in Caracas, Venezuela. You could say it was my doing, the youngest of the flock venturing out straightaway and then helping my siblings to follow.

I wanted to make the event everything my mother wanted. I knew that there would be relatives from near and far. Thomas was my mother's younger brother. He and his wife, Kirstine, lived on a big farm near Fjelstrup. They erected a tent in their large garden, big enough for forty guests to dine. I remembered my own childhood and how these affairs could go on and on. The womenfolk would gather in the parlors while the men went outside to inspect the barns or the crops, or perhaps went to the library to smoke and argue politics.

I explained everything to my girls, and I made a game of rehearsing Danish country manners. I sat on a chair, pretending to be a lady guest. As the girls lined up before me, they were to extend a hand, look at me, smile, and curtsy. Since they spoke no Danish, not even the greeting, *god-dag*, I instructed them to say hello in English.

The girls loved practicing and looked forward to the adventure of a big party in a faraway land.

Soon after our arrival the day came, and we donned our finery, piled into our VW bus, and headed for the farm. We left little John at home with a babysitter. As I had anticipated, the ladies were indeed sitting around in the parlors visiting.

Just before my mother led her granddaughters in, I gave them last minute reminders. One by one they were introduced, each of them behaving exactly true to their lessons. Karen, as the eldest, led the parade. You would have thought she had done this all her life! Ellen and Nina followed her example, putting out their hands, curtsying so nicely, making eye contact, saying hello, all just as we had practiced.

My three little American children truly won the hearts of all those Danish ladies. This may sound old-fashioned and hardly worth telling now, but then, as I saw the tears of pride and joy in my mother's face, I was so proud of my children, and so happy that we had taken the trouble to prepare for this time. For so many years she had shared other people's pleasures, exclaimed at their grandchildren. Now she had the joy of her own shining moment.

The dinner was a wonderful experience for the girls, too, and they often talked about it later in their lives. They were seated at a special table for children, as was the custom. I had told them to expect four courses: appetizer, soup, main dish, dessert.

A special cook and several helpers had been working in the old-fashioned kitchen for several days. There was no refrigeration in those days, and everything was cooked on a large woodstove. With no electric mixers or electric pots, no special gadgets or time-savers, those women turned out a predictably expansive and festive dinner.

First there was chicken in a cream sauce with the white asparagus tips one finds in Europe. It was served in delicate pastry shells. I knew the girls liked that.

The second course was one of my all-time favorites, Danish dumpling soup. On an occasion such as this, there would be three kinds of tiny dumplings: meat, bread, and so-called white dumplings, a flour-egg kind. Rice cooked with raisins was pressed into small individual molds and added to the soup by each guest. I had made this for my own family at home and I knew my girls liked it as much as I did.

Grandma's house.

The main course in this case was pork and beef roast. To serve only one kind of meat would not have been proper. The meat course was served with several kinds of vegetables, two kinds of potatoes—boiled white ones with brown gravy and small caramelized ones that mark the fancy Danish dinner. There were garnishes such as homemade spiced apple rings or pear preserves, and as always, sour cucumber salad. Bread, however, is not served with Danish dinners.

Dessert was the grand finale—homemade ice cream served with preserved fruits and macaroons. Making ice cream was a cook's real test. Concocted of rich cream, eggs, sugar, and vanilla, it was frozen in buckets set in large tubs filled with rock salt, ice (from the local dairy), and water. To make the ice cream smooth, you had to stir it often. I can well remember one cook who worked for my mother breaking into tears because her ice cream crystallized!

A French white wine was served with the first two courses, and a French red wine was served with the meats. Madeira wine from Spain accompanied the dessert. Between courses, trays of cigarettes and cigars were passed around. No worrying about lung cancer in those days!

The children had soda and fruit punch at their table. I had told my daughters, "Try a little of everything, and stay at the table until the dinner is over." They did as I said, all through the long long dinner, the speeches and singing and smoking, without a word of complaint, even though they did not understand a syllable of what was said. Afterwards they told me that the only thing they had not liked was the sour cucumber salad.

Ah, but the dinner wasn't quite done. During the long festivities, the cook had been busy in the kitchen baking a wonderful, rich coffee cake. This was an important distinction among cooks; each wanted to be known for her coffee cake. It was served along with a variety of homemade cookies and coffee, taken in the different parlors.

My aunt and uncle's celebration was an introduction for Karen, Ellen, and Nina to a different world, one I had told them about. For them, it was like stepping back in time to join that little girl, Solveig, in the small town of Fjelstrup in the beautiful country of Denmark.

On the Road

In the old tale called "Stone Soup," some vagabonds drift into town. They have nothing to eat, so they make a fire, fill a pot with water, and throw in stones to boil. As the townsfolk gather, they see a soup in the making, and they run home for something to add to the pot. They add bones, potatoes, onions, carrots, and barley. In the end, the vagrants' stone soup is tasty and nutritious, with enough for everyone, thanks to the goodwill of the townspeople.

I thought of that story as our family looked for a suitable home for our year in Denmark. So many people made the wheels turn for us. First we found an apartment in Haderslev, about eight miles from Fjelstrup. Haderslev is a larger town with about forty-five thousand inhabitants, a more convenient place for us, and one that resembled in many ways our home, Downers Grove, Illinois. Haderslev had beautiful parks and lakes, good schools and a library, and interesting stores. It is a very old town, dating back to the year 400. The large cathedral in the middle of town dates back to 1440, before Columbus landed in America. Some of the narrow streets still have cobblestones. Karen, Ellen, and Nina seemed to find all this fascinating and in some way familiar and comfortable.

*Haderslev's
cathedral.*

Our apartment was on the outskirts of town, one of four units in a building. The whole time we lived there, the other three apartments remained unoccupied. We found the place comfortable, with its large living room, two bedrooms, and modern kitchen and bath, although, being new, it seemed especially bare.

That was when our many friends began to make stone soup!

*Our apartment
in Haderslev.*

John with his friend Maren.

In Fjelstrup, friends and neighbors searched basements and lofts, and within a few days, they had gathered enough furniture, beds, bedding, lamps, dishes, pots, and pans to furnish our place. One of my father's friends, a man in the furniture business, gave us a used sofa that was fine, except for being very ugly! From Grandmother's loft we received a homely rug. All put together, though, the hand-me-downs and loaners made a home for us.

The girls went to school nearby, and John found a playmate just across the yard. The other child, a little girl, was from Belgium. Neither of them could speak much of anything, since they were not yet two years old. She did teach him to say "filo" for tricycle, and he taught her to say "Okay" American style, and they got along just fine. In my VW bus I trekked out to a junkyard and found a large tractor tire. I hauled white sand from the beach in buckets and garbage cans and made a great sandbox for our little United Nations group. A little Danish girl, Maren, soon joined the other two.

The three of them were ingenious. I received some complaints when little fingertips dug into the one-pound butter packages left at the doors by the milkman. I replaced the butter, and after that, the housewives watched for deliveries and brought the butter in before our little scavengers appeared.

On their way to school, the girls had to walk some streets and go through a small park, but the exciting part was walking under a busy street through a tunnel. At first, school was hard for them, but in a couple of months, they learned enough Danish to get along in the classroom and to make friends. I enrolled them in dancing classes, and they explored the old town and enjoyed playing in the beautiful parks.

Even as their language skills rapidly improved and they began to speak freely to their relatives and friends, they never spoke Danish in the apartment. Once they entered our door, they were Americans, and there was no cajoling them from English.

Small John called all his sisters Nina. I don't know if that was because Nina was the youngest girl, closest to him in age, or if it was simply convenient. Maybe there were too many languages coming at him all at once (English, Danish, Flemish, German on the rented TV, and some strange local dialect as well). His little brain must have been on overload.

The girls discovered books at the library that were in English, but the best times were when an American movie came on TV, and even better, the *I Love Lucy Show*.

Every Saturday we piled into our bus for a trip to the grandparents' house. Grandma Martha made all the foods they loved best, especially their favorite chocolate cake and small round pancake balls called *aebleskivers* that were served with her homemade jams. She knitted caps, gloves, and scarves for them and in general was the wonderful, loving grandmother they had not known before. A strong bond developed between young and old despite the initial language barrier. Grandpa took small John down long walks along the country roads. They could be seen walking slowly, hand in hand, the little boy talking, gesturing, pointing here and there, while Grandpa nodded agreeably despite the fact that he couldn't understand a word of it. Neither tired of their special time, and they went out on every visit. The girls learned the dialect spoken in South Jutland, to the delight of their old relatives and their own pleasure, too.

Of course we wanted to see Denmark, a country whose history goes back thousands of years, whose flag is the oldest in Europe. I wanted to show my children the white, sandy beaches, the rolling countryside, stately old castles, windmills and farms. They had boundless energy and curiosity, and our excursions were more than the old folks could do. Luckily, newfound friends, the Petersens, stepped in. Owin Petersen had a brother, Werner, who lived with his family a short block from our first home in Downers Grove. So of course they urged us to contact their relatives in Denmark, and in this way we made a friendship that has lasted a lifetime. Karla Petersen and I did our shopping together every week, and on Sundays we packed picnic baskets for our outings. Their two children, Owin Jr. and Liala, fell right in with the American girls and taught them a lot of Danish. Two-year-old John was perhaps the greatest benefactor.

Never having known his father, he thrived on the love and attention big Owin generously showered on him.

We went about in my car. Owin did not own a car, but he loved to drive, and we shared the task.

Together we toured the ancient towns of Ribe, Tønder, Kolding, and the beautiful castles and parks. We crossed the bridge to the island of Fyen and visited Hans Christian's tiny house in Odense. We frolicked in the waves at the beaches, and for extra adventure, we brought our passports and drove the fifty kilometers south to Germany where we could get cheap chocolate and other specialties.

Most people don't know that our American Independence Day is also celebrated in Denmark every year on the fourth of July as a tribute to the bond of friendship between our two countries. The celebration is held in the Rebild Bakker (hills) in central Jutland. Nature has shaped the heather-covered hills in such a way that they form a natural amphitheater. The steep hills turning into a flat plateau in the middle makes it a perfect setting for the planeloads of Danish-American immigrants who return every year, along with thousands of Danes who flock there as well. Dignitaries from both countries show up to give speeches and participate in the celebration.

In 1966, when we attended, Mayor Wagner from New York City was the keynote speaker. The young Princess Benedikte gave a short address, as did some Danish politicians. An American military band came up from Germany and was joined by the Danish Royal Military band from Copenhagen. It was a stirring moment when the "Star-Spangled Banner" was played while the Stars and Stripes were hoisted up one of the tall flagpoles, followed by the Danish flag, the Dannebrog, up a second pole, while the "Det er et yndigt Land" (This is a lovely land) played.

I had plans to see the surrounding countries as well. I read to my children about the histories of Germany, Holland, Belgium, France and England. When we traveled to those countries, the girls were aware of many changes that occurred as soon as we crossed borders. Most noticeable, of course, were the money and the language, but the landscape and architecture were also different. The canals of Amsterdam and the long dikes built by the Dutch to hold back the powerful sea fascinated them. In southwest

America's Independence Day is celebrated in Denmark.

Holland at a place called Walcheren, one of the dikes was purposely broken during World War II to keep the German army from stealing all the food grown there. I told my children about the Dutch children who were sent to Denmark after the war and placed in Danish homes where they could get the food and medical care they needed so badly. One of those children stayed in my parents' home. Her name is Clazina. She was sick with malaria and terribly undernourished, and a very sad little girl besides, but within a year she became a healthy, happy young person.

In Belgium there was another town with canals called Brugge. There we feasted on real Belgian waffles with strawberries and whipped cream. But our true destination was London.

We reached the ferry site in Folkestone one early evening and quickly decided to take one of the last available spaces for our car, even though we would arrive in England late at night. This turned out to be one of the few times that I, the otherwise gutsy mother, was truly frightened. I was guided onto the boat and up a ramp that seemed to go straight into the air. Horrified, I felt the wheels spinning on the greasy tracks, and the thought of the motor stalling and the car rolling backward absolutely boggled my mind. No one uttered a single sound in that car, neither my children nor my childhood friend Else, who had come along for the ride. It was as if we held one collective breath. Even when we had rolled into the assigned parking space and turned off the engine, we sat in silence, gathering our wits.

When we reached the English shore, we had to drive on the wrong side of narrow country roads to the campsite I had spotted on my map, and that was difficult and scary, but it was nothing after that vertical climb on the ferry boat.

The next morning we woke up to discover that we had parked right next to the bath house in a reserved space. No one seemed to care, but when I went into the camp store they did tease me about taking such a convenient spot. I returned to the bus lugging the same heavy, soggy bread I had eaten every day of my two-year stay in London twenty years before. It was comforting to find that some things never change.

We drove into London and spent five days visiting famous sites. We saw the guard change at Buckingham Palace, with all its fanfare. We saw the museum with the fancy crown jewels and watched people on boxes at the Marble Arch, yelling about the problems of the world, as they always had. We had tea and cakes at Lyons Tea house in Piccadilly Circus, and of course we saw Madame Toussaud's Wax Museum. Like every other tourist, we rode on

Cooking beside the camper.

double-decker buses, and we took underground trains to Kew Garden and on to Hempstead Heath. At day's end we headed for the outskirts of London, and with the help of some friendly "bobbies," we always managed to find a camping spot for the night.

When we finally turned back toward Denmark, the girls knew a lot about many places, but they had learned something even more valuable. They had survival skills; they knew how to make the best of a situation. The only thing that kept our tour from perfection was little brother John's absence. We had left him with our friends Karla and Owin, where he was so comfortable, but we sorely missed him. We had been without a father for not quite two years, and we were a tightly knit group, very interdependent, and the baby was in many ways our focal point. We needed him to be complete as a family.

As we neared Denmark, the girls urged me to drive faster. "We want to get there before John goes to bed," they said. "Don't stop for anything on the way."

We reached Haderslev before John's bedtime, but when we walked into Karla's house, he was so overwhelmed by all of us that he clung to her. His three sisters were near crying, thinking that he had forgotten us, his real sisters and mother. We decided right then and there that the next time we took a trip, we would take John, no matter what. We needed one another, every one, and that meant John, too.

Another Parting

That first night in Fjelstrup, lying in my grandparents' bed, I knew I had made the right decision, bringing the children to my childhood home. I needed the solace and strength of my devoted parents, and the children needed to trust that our lives would go on as a family, despite the terrible loss of their father. I was still grieving for Ray, but in this place I was drawing sustenance, like a wounded child. Every day I got up and made the day solid and dependable, even as I sought new experiences for my children, too. Somehow, the combination of familiarity and novelty was exactly right, and all of us grew.

Christmas 1965

DEAR FRIENDS!

It is now almost seven months since we came to Denmark and we do not need to look at the calender to know that Christmas is coming nearer. The snow has been falling on and of for several weeks and the days are barely eight hours long.

So, during these long winternights we sit back and talk about the marvelous summer we have had. Being here has been a wonderfull experience for us all, and we have many happy memories to take back with us next May.

I have had time to renew friendships with people I have not seen for many years and we have seen things and places which were dear to me during my childhood and youth. We have taken trips in our Volks-Wagen bus to England and Norway and seen much along the way and of-course we have crossed Denmark in all directions, and the children have learned much.

But, best of all, we have had a lovely time with the Grandparents. Even now when we live in our own apartment we get together with them two or three times a week and we now look forward to spending a real danish Christmas together with them. This will be the first Christmas they have ever had with Grandchildren around them.

Karen, Ellen and Nina are now big enough to do their own Christmas-shopping and they really enjoy looking at all the different things in the Danish stores. I think we all concentrate on little brother John, he is now $2\frac{1}{2}$ and beginning to know what it is all about.

So, we hope each and everyone of you will have as lovely a Christmas as we are looking forward to.

We send our very best regards to all and the best wishes for a blessed new year.

Solveig Hirsch,
Karen, Ellen, Nina and John

The time came, of course, when we had to return to "real life" in the United States. For the children, America was home, and they would not be entirely themselves until they were once again American children.

We had a big job, emptying the apartment and returning all the borrowed furniture and household items. Piling it all in our bus and hauling it back to lofts and basements provided comic relief again and again as those generous people expressed dismay at the sight of their old junk! They had not missed the items; in fact, they had appreciated the storage space.

In a different emotional vein, we had to untie the heartstrings my parents had tied around all of us. We were so close to them, and more, to family and friends who had become special to us over the twelve months.

My father insisted on coming with me as I drove to the harbor of Hamburg, Germany, to deliver our bus to a shipping company. They would transport it to New York along with a crate of clothes and purchases from our year.

We arranged to stay in a Manhattan hotel on arrival and confirmed our tickets. Step by step the day of our departure drew closer. I could see the excitement in the children's faces even as I was painfully aware of the strain on those of my mother and father. When we finally boarded the plane and took off, I felt keenly their loss; through the little oval plane window I caught a last look at their tense, pale faces. They looked as if they wanted to grab the plane and hold it back. I could only think that now they had memories of all of us, that they knew the children, and that although there was pain in that, there was joy, too.

Of course I wanted to get the fullest possible experience out of our return. I arranged to ship the car to New York so that we could drive to Chicago, even though shipping through the St. Lawrence Canal would not have added to my cost.

I wrote letters to friends and family who lived along the route, and we stayed in homes in Darien, Connecticut, Washington D.C., Pittsburgh, Pennsylvania, and Springfield, Ohio. My childhood friend, Else, decided to come along to keep me company again, and to see the United States.

All my work in arranging details paid off, both because it kept me focused so that I did not over-identify with my parents' anxiety, and because I knew everything would go smoothly and give my children more happy times.

In New York I left Else, who spoke no English, in the hotel with my kids while I made my way to Hoboken, New Jersey, to locate the car. That homely, dirty gray bus was like an old relative. The side mirror was broken, but otherwise it had traveled well.

We drove out to Montclair, New Jersey, to visit the Slaters, who had hosted me as an *au pair* in 1949. I was greeted as a long lost daughter. We renewed the memories of my wedding to Ray. It had been December, quite cold, and the Slaters had come all the way on the train so that Mr. Slater could walk me up the aisle in the Nebo Lutheran Church.

We drove on to Washington and saw the Capitol and the White House, monuments, and the grave of President Kennedy, another young father who had died just two weeks before ours. We drove across Pennsylvania and Ohio uneventfully, but when I reached Chicago, I lost my way and got my welcome home in the form of flashing lights on top of a highway patrol car. With all that we had accomplished, and all the emotional storms we had weathered, that last straw unglued me. I stood in front of our dusty bus next to the police officer and cried big, hot, frustrated tears. He studied me for a moment, glancing over at the busload of children, and in the end, he told me sternly that I must never again make an illegal U-turn on an interstate highway, and he sent me on my way with a warning written on a slip of paper.

Home

In a couple of weeks, we had left Europe, then crossed the ocean and half of a continent. My little girls, Karen, Ellen, and Nina, delighted in rediscovering their old belongings and the tight little house we had lived in for such a short time before our trip. Quickly they were again in their circle of friends. Little John, now two and a half, ran across the street and courageously faced the rough Bostwick and McIntyre boys. We were home. Our long sojourn abroad had been right for us—for me, for the children, for our hearts. All of us had learned and grown, and of course I could not put a price on what it meant to my parents, but most of all, the year had been a long process in which we had become this new family of five.

6

NEW BEGINNINGS
An End to Loneliness

After Denmark: Creating a New Life in Downers Grove

In the months that followed our return from Denmark, we set about getting reestablished in our town and neighborhood. The girls were enrolled in the choir at the Congregational Church, and I signed them up for piano lessons. Our name finally came up on the waiting list at the Fairview Pool Association, to the great delight of my children. Not only could they swim every day and take lessons, they also reunited with their friends and made new ones at the pool. John, now three years old, was wary of the noise and splashing, and only after I promised that I would never, ever dunk him did he let me carry him back and forth in the shallow end. With his arms wound tightly around my neck and his legs around my waist, we slowly wandered back and forth, back and forth, much to the amusement of the lifeguards. After a few weeks he built up enough nerve to splash his feet, and a few weeks after that, he let me dunk him in the water—still holding onto my neck, of course. Predictably, by summer's end he was totally confident in and out and under the water, his eyes red from the chlorine. The Florida grandparents came visiting and fawned over the courageous little boy.

One Sunday morning after church we stopped at the Ogden Pet and Feed Store to look at a hamster, and less than an hour later we drove home with a new pet—but not a hamster. Instead, we took home a little puppy with a curly black coat and big brown eyes. We named her Nellie.

Nellie.

We were settling in and in many ways seemed a typical all-American family, except that one important thing was missing: no father came home from work at the end of the day as in other families on our street. No father made trips to the hardware store and then puttered around the house on weekends. We were missing something very important, and the loss was permanent.

But life had to go on, and as is my way, I kept us busy. I studied the Chicago papers for events that would interest my children, and things began to open up. Sunday came around and we piled in the car and went to exhibits at the Museum of Science and Industry, the Lincoln Park Zoo, the Shedd Aquarium, the flower show. There were plentiful opportunities. I studied the paper on Fridays; on Sunday morning, we voted on where to go—majority ruling, of course. Whenever possible we took along Mrs. Atkinson, an elderly widowed lady who lived a few houses away. She became our adopted grandmother.

Another girl, Mary Petersen, came into our family. She lived across the street and was right between Karen and Ellen in age. Eventually we packed our camping gear and accompanied the Petersen family to a Wisconsin campground near Mauston. Bob Petersen had a boat, and he taught all of us to water-ski. Unfortunately, Mary's mother had health problems, so although she accompanied us, she did not participate in many activities. Mary and her sister, Roberta, loved having playmates right in the next campsite, and Bob grew close to my family, especially to John.

Our weekends ceased being gloomy as we learned to be resourceful and to take advantage of opportunities that came along. Once school started, the girls got involved in a Brownie troop and Sunday school. To make John feel secure, I got involved in what was called the "Picture Lady" program at the children's school and was assigned to his class. This program entailed teaching kids about art and sculpture once a month. I also joined a bridge group, and I went to social events held locally. During the winter, I took classes for adults held at the nearby high school.

I planned my life carefully around my little family and figured that once John went to school I would apply for a job within the school system as a kitchen helper, janitor, or perhaps an assistant to the librarian—anything that would give me an insurance and retirement program and afford me the same hours off as my children. Meanwhile, I let it be known among friends who often worked as substitute teachers that I would baby-sit for their small children. This provided John with playmates and helped me earn enough money to pay for groceries.

Eventually, after three years of widowhood and some pressure from fellow church members, I agreed to join a social group for single parents raising children alone. The meetings usually presented a speaker who talked about the problems of being the sole parent, and they were held in a church basement in nearby Hinsdale. Picnics and outings were held for families, and dinner dances and bowling parties were arranged for the adults.

I found it difficult to go out as a single person after having had a marriage partner for thirteen years. I felt as if I were being unfaithful to my husband. But my friends persisted, and after some months, I fell in with the group. When the election for new officers came up, I was asked to be the membership chairperson.

As such, I was to meet the man who would soon change my life. He stepped through the door looking as hesitant and uncomfortable as I had felt the first time I attended. Falling right into my new role-to-be as membership coordinator, I greeted him and introduced myself. He signed his name on the guest list: *Jake Sedlet.* Before the meeting started, he told me that he had not gone out alone for many years. His wife had died after a long bout with cancer, and he and his son, Steve, were now left in the house alone. His daughter, Susan, was away at college.

After the speaker finished, I introduced Jake to some of the other members of the group. We served coffee and cookies and told him about upcoming plans. The group's next event was a "Sadie Hawkins" party to be held in someone's home. It was a dress-up party, and Jake said he doubted that he would attend. He came to the next meeting, though, and the subject of the party came up again. He asked if I had dressed as Daisy Mae, and he found it amusing when I laughingly said that I was hardly equipped for the role.

Our next meeting was an installation dinner held at a restaurant on Roosevelt Road in Lombard. I was standing by the piano singing with a group of friends when Jake arrived. I went over to greet him and assured him that his son must be happy to see him getting on with his life. Children worry about their parents. He admitted that Steve had encouraged him to come.

He smiled. "Besides, you told me I must come, so I did."

I explained that I couldn't keep him company at dinner, as I was sitting at the head table with other newly elected officers.

"That's all right," he said. "As long as you promise to have a drink with me afterwards."

So it was that we later found ourselves at a small table in the back of the restaurant. Conversation came easily as we shared concerns for our children and talked about the sorrowful experience of losing our mates. The time passed so quickly that we failed to notice everyone else in our party leaving. At the car, Jake said he would like to see me again soon, and I just told him that my name was in the phone book.

At a church meeting the next week I told some friends about Jake. They knew him both as a former neighbor and a fellow employee and liked him a lot. A few days later he called to invite me to dinner in Chicago. My friends took matters into their own hands, however, and invited us to their home for bridge. We postponed dinner and played bridge instead.

The day he picked me up to go to the Chicago restaurant was the fourth of April, his birthday. It was also the day Martin Luther King was shot in Memphis, Tennessee. When I went into the ladies' lounge I found a black woman crying. As I offered her comfort, she was the one to break the news. "They killed our king," was what she said, and we grieved together.

Nevertheless, the evening with Jake was a happy one for me. He had told

  me it was his birthday, and to make it a little special, I had brought a nice card and a tiny tiepin, nothing too personal. After dinner we walked to a nearby

Jake and Solveig begin to date.

movie theatre. We saw a French movie—appropriately enough, *A Man and a Woman*. For such a shy man, he surprised me by taking my hand as the show began. He said he thought that was what we were supposed to do in a movie theatre. At my door, I assured him that I had had a lovely evening, but I did not invite him in. Being a single mother of four young kids made me cautious even with the nicest people.

Quickly, however, it became obvious that our relationship would not remain casual. In fact, the very next day, he sent me twelve perfect red roses with a note thanking me for a wonderful evening.

In the months that followed, we discovered that if we were together, each of us could put our past behind us and learn to care for another person. Neither of us wanted to live alone. We wanted our children to have as good a family life as we could give them. And so, before the next school year began, our two families got to know each other, and we started a new life.

Blending

We spent the summer months bringing our families together and trying to make our plans fit into the time slot before the new school year began. It was not easy. Jake lived at the south end of our town and we lived at the north end. There were two school systems to consider, with five kids moving up the ranks. It would be Karen's first year in high school and Ellen's first in junior high. Nina would enter sixth grade, and John was new to kindergarten.

My group had been faced with many adjustments during the past five years. We had moved from St. Louis, Missouri, where all three girls were born, and within the next few months they had not only gained a baby brother, but they had also lost their kind, loving father. Some months later we had again moved, to a smaller, more manageable house in another neighborhood. Then, to top it off, at the end of the school year, we had packed up and flown to Denmark to spend a year where they were in a new school in a new country, learning to speak a new language. Now, they had to learn to share their mom not only with a new father, but with two new siblings as well.

On one hand they were quite excited. They were so happy for John that he would finally have a daddy. On the other hand, they grieved over losing their friends in the school and neighborhood. Karen seemed to take it the hardest. She had looked forward to entering high school with her friends from junior high. My strong, courageous girl began to buckle. We talked and cried as we weighed possibilities together. She wanted me to be happy, but she also dreaded another change.

And Steve and Susan were hesitant about getting a stepmother. They would have to adjust to four step-siblings and, of course, share their father. Susan, the elder child in that family, had the most difficult time. She was only eighteen and had not had enough time to grieve over her mother's illness and death. She had difficulties adjusting to being away at college. After her first year, Jake had moved her from the big state school in Normal to a smaller private school, Bradley University in Peoria. When she came home for spring vacation and learned that her father was dating, she wasn't ready for it. She knew that Jake and Steve were lonely, and that they had problems with housekeeping and their sense of abandonment. Still, having a new person in her life was too hard. She lashed out at her father, and it fell to Steve, younger by four years, to take her aside and convince her that this was the best thing for them all, that their good father did not deserve an empty, sad life. In just three years, Steve would be leaving for college himself, and he looked ahead to the day when he would pack up and leave his father behind; he didn't want to leave him all alone. Eventually all of the older children came to agree that it was good to see their lonely parents so happy.

But I wondered how this decision was affecting John. He had often implored me to go to a store and find a new daddy. But he also thought he might see his father if he climbed to the top of the tree in our backyard— or that he could send a message to God to fix our daddy and send him back to us. I wanted to choose just the right moment to tell him he was getting a new daddy. It came one day when he was sitting on the clothes hamper watching me fix my hair. Once again he was talking about getting us a dad like the other neighborhood boys had. I knew I had to tell him what was happening. I said, "John, Mr. Sedlet has agreed to be our dad."

Just like that, he knew, and it was so simple. I would never have guessed his reaction. Without saying a word to me, he jumped off the hamper and ran, hopped, and skipped through the house happily shouting, "We're getting a daddy! We're getting a daddy!" I was surprised, and of course I was delighted. Then the phone rang, and his reaction was even more surprising. He grabbed for the phone; when he heard Jake's voice he spontaneously yelled, "Hello, Daddy!" I was embarrassed, but Jake quickly gathered his wits and said, "Hello, Son."

We were sure that we had made the right decision. We did not want to live without each other, but housing and school situations hovered over us and made us feel everything was speeding along too fast. There was so much to do in a short time.

We wanted house-hunting to be a family affair, so when Jake and I saw a place that seemed suitable, we insisted that all six kids come along and voice their opinion. In hindsight I realize that we must have been the real estate person's worst nightmare, but this process set the pattern for doing things in a democratic way, and we followed it whenever possible.

Actually, I found the house on 57th Street quite by accident. A disagreement between our real estate person and the seller originally kept her from showing it to us, but once we found it and liked it, we sold our two smaller houses and bought it. The pool we belonged to was right behind our back fence, and the YMCA and schools were nearby as well. For John, the best part was the old farm behind us. It had horses, geese, chickens, and other animals, and to top it off, there were two boys who lived nearby, one his age, Jamie, and his younger brother, Little John, so he had playmates from day one. We bought the house and moved in—before school started and two weeks before we were married!

Fitting everybody in the house took some thinking. We divided up the rooms by age. Susan and Karen were the oldest girls, so we put them in one room and let Nina and Ellen share another. John slept in a small room next to our bedroom, and Steve was happy to move into the large finished basement room. At first I worried that he would feel abandoned by himself—he was only fifteen. But he assured me it was a great deal, with space for his hobbies, his ping pong table, and the privacy to practice his guitar and visit with his friends. And it was definitely better than sharing a room with a five-year-old.

The 57th Street house.

We distributed furniture however it seemed practical, with the overflow stored in the garage. You could call our interior décor "eclectic," to use a popular term, though a more fitting one would be "Early Salvation Army style." Our big hurdle was to find a dining room table big enough to seat all eight of us. Temporarily we used half the ping pong table, covering it with a bed sheet. Around this rickety substitute we held some serious discussions. One was to decide whether we should get a square or circular table. True to his scientific disposition, Jake calculated which would give us the most square inches to the perimeter, and spoke in favor of the square. He was right about inches, but I argued that a circle was much better for communication and eye contact, and when the subject came up for a vote, round won out. We set forth to purchase the largest one we could find, and what we bought seemed enormous in the store. Once it was in place in our family room, though, we had to put the extra leaf in to make it big enough for us and guests.

The changes involved in joining our families and moving to a new house were a strain on everyone, but as the summer wore on and we all got to know one another, even Susan, the child who was most reluctant to accept the changes, got swept up in the excitement. She bought a pretty pink dress for the wedding and settled into our new house.

A Wedding Day

Getting the pink dress for Susan was the least of our preparations. Five other kids needed outfits, and a million other things had to be done. We had moved into the big house less than two weeks before our wedding date. To keep things right and proper, Jake slept on a cot downstairs in Steve's room. Furniture and household goods were spread all over, and two days before the wedding we had a new king-size bed delivered. I ordered a blue dress and a pillbox hat to match. My only problem was shoes—I found the perfect color, but they were a size too big. Some tissues stuffed into the toes took care of that. Jake bought two new suits, one brown and one dark blue. He planned to wear the brown one until he found out about my choice of a blue dress.

He later told me that he had also bought a complete set of new underwear, figuring he had to make a good impression on our wedding night. After that, he said, the old stuff would just have to do!

Karen and Ellen chose to wear yellow silk dresses handed down from our lawyer's daughter, Leslie. But we were stuck when it came to finding a dress for our little blond Nina. Nothing was right, neither size- nor price-wise. Quickly we bought a few yards of dotted swiss and a pattern and set Karen up in the corner of the dining room with the old sewing machine I had bought at Sears to sew her baby clothes on some fifteen years before.

She cut and measured and stitched, and in less than two days, Nina had a beautiful white dress trimmed with yellow daisies. I have that little dress tucked away in a drawer, and it brings a smile to my face whenever I see it.

Steve was all right in his sports jacket and his father's shirt and tie, and late one evening I shortened little John's pants.

The big day arrived, and we had to be at the church at four. But as in every normal family, there were breakfast and lunch to think about, and were we out of milk! People stopped by, the telephone rang, and Bucky the dog had to be bailed out of doggie jail. But somehow it all happened. The guests left, the kids helped each other get dressed, and they left in the old rusty blue car. Finally Jake and I drove down 55th Street, then down Maple Avenue and Curtiss Street to the Congregational Church. Pastor Cook had agreed to adapt the service to fit our Jewish and Protestant religions.

We did not talk much, but as I sat in that car, next to the man I had come to love so much in such a short time, I was fully aware of entering a new stage in my life. As I had at other times—when I first stepped onto the airplane and flew to London, or when the Swedish boat carried me across the Atlantic Ocean to a new world and I drove through the tunnel into New Jersey—I now faced an entirely new stage in my life. After my five years of widowhood and independence, I was challenged with making a good and happy and balanced home for our combined families.

We met with our kids in the church parlor. We pinned flowers on each other and went through some formalities. As we stood by the church door I heard the organ play, and my friend Madeline sang "Solveig's Song," by Edvard Grieg.

Our kids stood around us in front of Pastor Cook, and when the tears drowned my voice he gently guided me through the words: "For better or worse—till death do you part." I had said them before with Ray. I had thought that marriage was forever, and now with Jake holding my hands I couldn't face that I might ever lose him.

The day went on: We had a room to ourselves at the Willoway Manor restaurant—just us and a few relatives. It was over, and we were committed to each other—all of us. Our day ended on a comical note. One by one the other kids went to bed, but Susan still sat with Jake and me in the living room. We did not want to leave her sitting alone. We felt uneasy telling her that all we wanted to do was to go to our room, close our door, and hold each other in our new king-size bed forevermore.

We Settle In

Once the younger group started school, Susan and I were at home facing one another and the job of getting her ready to return to Bradley. I did not want to push her, and she could not get herself to seek my help. Again I

followed my own mother's advice—when you see something that needs doing, just do it. So, in the end, I went down into the basement one day and started sorting, washing, and mending her clothes. I wasn't going to nag her and make her feel inadequate, with all the adjustments she had had to deal with. But I could sew on buttons.

We did not talk about my doing this, but one day, when the boxes were filled and everything was in order, Susan came down into the basement. We made some small talk, and then from behind her back she pulled a lovely long-stemmed red rose, her way of showing her appreciation. Without knowing it, she had followed her father's example in giving me flowers, as he had done after our first date, when I had left him standing on my doorstep.

As the weeks went by, it was around our big round table that most of the important decisions were made, such as the division of labor. I agreed to take charge of shopping for food and cooking, and I volunteered to do all the laundry—as long as it was placed in the hamper or by the washing machine. Though this sounds simple, it took a while to work. Many was the morning I heard, "I don't have any socks/underwear/T-shirts!" I did not pick up clothes from under beds or those left on the floor or stuck in closets. It wasn't long before the lesson was learned. Other chores were divided up more or less democratically, although everyone had to be reminded more than once that there were six of them and only one of me—and no maid service. The kids washed dishes, fed the dogs and picked up after them on the lawn, took out trash, cleaned their own bedrooms and the showers, and so on. John got off the easiest, fairly enough, but he set the table and, eager to please, washed his hands— both sides!

We didn't allow TV or phone calls during dinner. I suppose some of the kids' friends were surprised the first time they heard, "Sorry, we're eating" before a hang-up, but everyone got used to it and dinner conversation was a lively time to share the adventures of our day. At one end of the room the wall was covered with books, so when discussions became contentious, someone usually popped up and found the appropriate reference source to settle the score right then and there.

I remember laughing when Steve told about a friend being so curious about the pretty girl who was accompanying him to school—nobody had seen her before. Steve, a sophomore, was going to school with kids he had known since kindergarten, while Karen, a brand new freshman, was also brand new to South High. Steve enjoyed withholding the information, saying, "Oh I just know her!" He strung his friends along for a while, then let slip the information that her name was Karen, and that he lived with her! He was so confident, believable, and cool that his gullible friends, blown away, could only ask, "Gee, Steve, do your parents know?" At that he just shrugged and walked away, saved by the bell.

Of course he didn't stop to think what his friends might think of Karen!

Traditions

I grew up with a deep appreciation for traditions, and I realized that in this new, blended family, there would be many things we hadn't shared—beliefs, legends, and customs that went back generations. The dictionary defines traditions as the handing down of beliefs, legends, customs, and so on from generation to generation, and we couldn't do that, so we built traditions as we went along.

Our new lives started in the fall with the beginning of the school year and the anticipation of our shared holidays, like Thanksgiving. I realize now that how we celebrated our first holidays together built the foundation for the rest of our years. I discovered at Thanksgiving that we enjoyed many of the same foods: turkey and all the side dishes (corn casserole, creamed onion, squash, green beans, two kinds of cranberry sauce, mashed and sweet potatoes, giblet and regular gravies). We had at least three kinds of pies, one of them pumpkin. It would take years for me to learn that nobody really liked pumpkin pie, and that Jake didn't like pie at all! We ate all that food because it was the American way, and it became *tradition.* One deviation from the Plymouth Rock gang was that we later added cheesecake and a chocolate whipped-cream torte.

In true pilgrim fashion, we always invited another family who, like us, had no close family nearby. Over the years, we hosted families from Holland, Belgium, Ethiopia, Israel, and sometimes people who just lived far from their loved ones in other parts of the United States. Jake's brother, Joe, his young wife, Donna, and their son, Paul, from Milwaukee became permanent fixtures at our Thanksgiving table. Paul was John's age. And there was always "Little Mary," who slid into our family when we lived in

our house on Washington Street. She had lived across the street, and her home was an unhappy, gloomy place, clouded by her mother's mental illness. Wherever we went, Mary was sure to go. She even followed us when I married Jake and moved to the house on 57th Street. Her constant presence prompted Susan to remark, "Just two more payments and Mary will be ours."

Little Mary.

Our first Christmas together.

For our Christmas feast we had standing rib roast and Yorkshire pudding, since ham did not fit with a Jewish group. I baked multitudes of cookies, breads, and fruitcakes, but sure enough, if any particular kind was missing, someone was bound to notice that small break with tradition. When Susan came home from college, I had the ingredients all ready for her to make rum balls from her mother's special recipe.

To this day I feel that the need for building our very own traditions had an important and deep meaning. In our case, it was the need to feel grounded and united. Jake was Jewish-Polish, and I am Scandinavian; of course, we had to concoct our own American traditions, as millions of immigrants from every corner of the earth have done throughout this country's history.

As the years rolled on and melded us into a cohesive unit, we celebrated both Christian and Jewish holidays, lighting Chanukah candles every night for a week while we decorated a Christmas tree. I learned from the Jewish Hagadah how to fix the Seder plate and meal for Passover, and soon afterward, we decorated Easter eggs with spring flowers and bunnies.

During the Christmas holidays we piled into the station wagon and took wreaths to two cemeteries to remember the two parents who had died. None of us wanted to leave them out of our memories, and by doing this together, in our new unit, we gave the old families and the lost parents a proper respect and a place in our boisterous family group.

On a different note, our blending of traditions even showed up in the matter of dogs. My family had faithful little black Nellie, and the Sedlets had Bucky. It was with Bucky that we saw that things couldn't remain the same. Bucky was a gentle soul who had provided immense comfort to the family during the long illness of Jake's wife, but after her death, he was inconsolable, and for months he was ever-wandering, looking for his mistress all over town. Police and neighbors had to bring him home, and when we moved into the new house, he was totally confused and there were many complaints about him. Jake took him to a place for wayward dogs. We hoped he would be adopted, although the chances were slim. Sadly, we never saw him again.

We did still have Nellie, but the kids were not going to settle for one dog; nothing less than two would do—tradition again. Without either parent knowing anything about it, they scoured the newspaper ads and with much secrecy found a German shepherd puppy in Midlothian, a town twenty miles south of Downers Grove. The pup was smuggled in through a powder room window and hidden in Steve's basement lair, not to be seen until Christmas morning. As a big box under the tree was unwrapped, a small dark head with pointed ears peeked out and we had a new family member who was with us for sixteen years. The kids assured us, "It's a mini-shepherd." They pointed out, too, that Nellie wouldn't be lonely now.

Well. Here are some points to consider.

1. Do not ever give a mother of six kids a puppy at six o'clock on Christmas morning.

2. There is no such thing as a mini-shepherd, as our vet confirmed. The pup weighed seventy-five pounds one year later.

3. As for Nellie, she was insulted and annoyed at the invasion of her territory by a bratty, nippy puppy, and she left the room anytime the pup came near.

So much for the tradition of two dogs. Nevertheless, the puppy did grow

Curry meets Nellie.

up to be a gorgeous golden-haired shepherd and I loved her almost as much as plain little Nellie. We named her Curry, after the spice that is a product of many different spices mixed together, a fitting name for a dog of numerous origins.

Great Expectations

For the first time since he was four months old, John had a father in the house, and a brother besides. He had been surrounded his whole life by four doting females, and all of us had loved him passionately. Now, though, he had men around, and after a few months, he saw that he wasn't being treated on equal terms.

His mommy was cutting his hair.

Of course, I had been cutting everyone's hair—his sisters', and even my own—just as I had learned to fix faucets and paint a house. And if I do say so, we all looked fine. But when I tried to convince little John of that, he begged to go to a real barbershop, "like Steve and Dad."

I drove him to the village and held his hand as we walked to Jim's Barbershop. There was a red, white, and blue rotating pole outside. Jim was reading a newspaper, sitting in one of his chairs. He perked up when we came in and installed John in a big chair with a booster seat. I watched in the mirror.

On the marble shelf in front of Jim were brushes and combs in a tall glass filled with a blue liquid. There were little snippers for the neckline, and others for nose-hairs. A cup with soap and a brush to lather men's beards. A strap to sharpen the long narrow knife used for scraping beards. On one end a long silver box held hot towels for after a shave, and there were creams, colognes, and aftershave lotions. In this men's salon, John was fascinated.

Jim put a round white scarf around John's neck, pumped up the chair, and began snipping. John's fine blond hair floated to the floor. He sat very still and quiet as Jim kept up a patter to accompany his cutting. In a little while, Jim brushed John's neck with a soft brush and straightened his shirt collar and praised him for being so good. He lowered the chair and out jumped John. I paid $2.50 and we went out onto the sidewalk.

Just down the corner was an old-fashioned soda fountain. Since this was a special occasion, I suggested a chocolate soda. He loved the stools at the counter there.

In front of the ice-cream store, I said, "Well, John, are you happy now that you've been to Dad and Steve's barbershop and had your hair cut by a barber?"

To my surprise, John took a long moment to reply and then, with shy hesitation, he said he wasn't really happy, no.

I squatted down to his eye level. "What's the matter?" I asked. "This is the very same barbershop. It's even the same chair where they sit. Whatever is wrong?"

He looked at me with his hazel-green eyes. He had such a sad little face.

"Mom," he said. "I wanted curls, like Dad and Steve have!"

Ellen's Exodus

I often heard Ellen say jokingly, "I'm the p-o-o-r middle child." I didn't believe that she felt left out or ignored, but at the same time, things said in jest sometimes have an undercurrent of meaning.

In the case of my Ellen, she had all her life lived in the shadow of her bright, efficient, protective sister, two years older. When their father died, ten-year-old Karen assumed a protective role not only toward Ellen, who was eight, but also toward six-year-old Nina and baby John. Even toward me, sometimes.

Five years later, when I remarried, Ellen acquired two more older siblings. Susan, at seventeen, had started college, but both Steve and Karen were established in high school, with top grades and lots of friends, when Ellen entered. I noticed that Ellen was a quiet one, a pretty girl who might benefit from a chance to shine on her own. She seemed young for a student exchange, but as I thought about it, I got the idea of working something out privately.

During my young years in Copenhagen, I had become friends with a lively, redheaded Norwegian girl named Bodil. We met when we were both working in day care centers. Eventually, of course, we parted ways, but

Solveig and Bodil.

our friendship endured. We married and had children at about the same times, and for fifty years we've written back and forth. So I thought of Bodil Beccer's family as a possible home away from home for my daughter, while we might host Bodil's daughter, Ellen Beccer. Both my Ellen and the Norwegian family were enthusiastic.

When I traveled to Denmark with my children, I also took them to visit the Beccers in Halden, in southeastern Norway, close to the Swedish border and Oslo fjord, so they were not wholly unfamiliar to Ellen. She had been ten then, but she remembered how beautiful the area was, with such high mountains.

Our main problem was juggling school-system schedules. It became obvious that we couldn't work it out for the girls to switch at the same time, and in the end, that was a good thing, because it gave my Ellen time to fit into the Beccer family (between two girls!), and it gave Ellen B. a solid base for coming to us a year later.

Ellen worked all summer—babysitting and clerking at Ma and Pa's Candy Store on Main (now long gone). She even painted a fence for the family next door. I sewed dresses and skirts and knitted wool mittens for the Nordic winter.

Her excitement never wavered, but I clearly remember Jake calling me in the middle of a workday to ask if I was really ready to send Ellen away for a whole year. He had been thinking about it all day, he said, worrying that I would miss her more than I knew. Actually, he was right, but how could I ask Ellen to give up her plans because I would miss her?

So the day came—July 21, 1971—and we steered the wagon to O'Hare Airport. At one moment I looked at Ellen: darkly tanned from her outdoors work, she was wearing an orange dress, and her beautiful green eyes seemed brighter than ever. I felt a surge in my stomach, knowing that she would be gone for a year in which I would not see her or be in charge of her life. I knew the house would be empty without her, but when she smiled, I smiled back.

Ellen's departure was a forerunner of what I came to think of as The Great Exodus. From 1968 until July 1971, when she left, we had had the joy of being one big family. Susan came home often from Peoria, and even with teen jobs and school activities, we seemed to gather at the big round table regularly.

From the beginning, I had been aware that time was short. Except for John, the kids were all nearer to adulthood than childhood, and I was determined to pack in as many family activities as we could. I managed to pull Jake, the reluctant camper, away from his desk for forays to Illinois, Wisconsin, and Michigan, and he enjoyed himself despite his misgivings. We went to state and county fairs, and during our first Easter, in 1969, we even booked a trip to Caracas, Venezuela, to visit my sister. She had a large house and a full-time maid, but when she saw us pouring out of the plane, she almost spun off into a fainting spell. I could see her whirling at the thought of the eight of us with her husband, two kids, and herself for a whole week, but we did just fine.

We toured in two cars. Jake drove a Mercedes belonging to my brother-in-law Lou Marcello. We learned all about Simon Bolivar, the great liberator of Venezuela, and we studied the country's history and

Ellen makes the news.

189

government. We traveled through mountains to Colonia Tovar, a remote Swiss village, and then, on our return trip, we stopped over at the Dutch islands of Curaçao and Aruba.

In 1970 we began visiting colleges and universities, as we would every year for some time. Steve wanted to escape Chicago winters. He did apply to the University of Illinois, Champaign, but he was also accepted to universities in New Mexico and Arizona, and I just couldn't think of sending a kid off to a school we hadn't even seen. So it was that we had one of the remarkable journeys of our lives.

During Easter vacation, 1971, all eight of us packed into our brown station wagon and headed southwest. Our clothes were stored in large roof-top containers. In the car, each person was allowed a pillow and one small bag for personal items. We had five licensed drivers: Jake, me, Susan, Steve, and Karen. We were able to drive fourteen hundred miles straight around the clock. Telling it, it sounds like a nightmare, but it was in fact hilarious. We had all discussed the possibility of ruining the trip with bitching and fighting, and we were all determined to have a great trip.

I packed a small cooler with two dozen hardboiled eggs, and a box of Fanny Mae chocolates for each person. After all, it was Easter.

I had assumed we would have a picnic, but in the barren deserts of New Mexico, the only green grass we found was inside a circle surrounding the state capitol in Santa Fe. Undaunted, we piled out. Nina tied a scarf around John's head to blindfold him while the rest of us hid the two dozen dyed eggs. Finding them wasn't a great challenge, since the green circle was small and the grass was sparse, but we weren't prepared for the terrific heat, and we discovered that the delicious Fanny Mae chocolates had melted into gooey gobs. We also didn't have any salt and pepper for the eggs.

Eating, in general, was a test of our ingenuity. For one thing, we found a huge range of prices. Jake became the decision maker. He would study the selections on the menu and then announce a limit for a particular meal, usually $1.00-1.25 for breakfast, half a dollar more for lunch, and then for dinner, $3.50 was the absolute limit. The kids were able to put together amazing meals without exceeding the limit. I recall Nina ordering two hot chocolates, one English muffin and a donut for breakfast, and leaving with a nickel to spare. Ellen, on the other hand, astonished a waitress by ordering a B.L.T. sandwich, hold the lettuce and tomato. It took the poor woman a few minutes to register that what Ellen wanted was a bacon sandwich!

Today the phrase for what we had might be *quality time.* Hanging together and making the very best of it. We did visit the two schools, and we met two friends of Jake's from his college days. We visited some Jewish friends who were celebrating Passover and who ate only matzo crackers with their meals. We visited the unique Indian village of Taos and shopped in Albuquerque. We drove up the mountain to the Los Alamos laboratory, where atomic bombs were assembled in great secrecy during World War II. Jake had a pleasant reunion with some of the people he had known during his involvement in that project's satellite site under the ball field of the University of Chicago.

We returned home stuffed with new impressions and feeling closer than ever. But Susan's last statement about the trip still rings in my ears. We were within a few miles of Downers Grove when she turned to Steve and said, "After all of this, if you decide to go to U of I Champaign, I think I will kill you!"

Well, Steve did.

And she didn't.

The Other Ellen

By the time the "other Ellen" arrived on a hot August day in 1973, the group around our table had diminished considerably. Susan had started her teaching career in Baltimore. Steve and Karen had started college at the University of Illinois, Champaign. Those empty spaces gaped at us.

Then came Ellen Beccer, a tall, blond Norwegian girl with a sunny disposition and a hearty laugh. Immediately, she felt like part of our household. As the months went by, Jake would ask her now and then, "Are you getting homesick yet?" To settle the issue once and for all, she finally told him that she was much too busy for such sentiments and if she ever had a bout of longing for Norway, she would be sure to let him know.

As a private exchange student over sixteen years old, she could get her driver's license. She made several mistakes, but I assume the testing officer was so distracted by her stunning blonde beauty that he overlooked

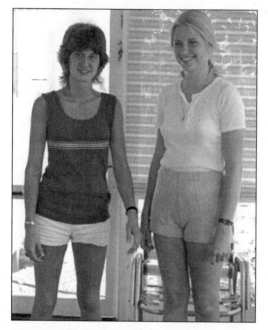

Ellen and Ellen.

them! After that she was able to drive our Chevrolet convertible, and she said she felt like a Hollywood movie star.

Ellen turned out to be a two-for-one deal. A Danish girl, Lene, had settled in with a family a few blocks away, and soon she was a frequent guest at our table. They were in classes together, talked on the phone incessantly, and spent a lot of time together.

Our Ellen took an after school job, as her siblings had done, to save money for college, but Ellen B., looking forward to a taxpayer-provided free education in Norway, had no such goals to meet. She seemed to dance her days away, and her enthusiasm was contagious. When we took her to Florida during spring vacation, her excitement at the sight of an orange tree made us all get out of the car so she could have a photograph taken of herself picking an orange. She reveled in the warm ocean and sandy beaches, so unlike the freezing waters and rocky shores of the Norwegian fjords. And of course Disney World was the ultimate.

Until we took her to Washington, D.C. This was in the days of the Watergate scandal. We sat in the gallery, watching the senators we had seen on TV. Ellen was experiencing history in the making. Then a guard at the White House quietly asked her, "Is it true that blondes have more fun?" and she wavered between feeling flattered and feeling insulted.

A Swedish AFS exchange student invited her to the prom, and we shopped for dresses for both Ellens. Ours had lost the pounds she gained in Norway, but our other Ellen so loved American food, she had gained more than twenty pounds over the winter. Still, we found dresses for both sizes. They walked around with their hair in big curlers on the day of the big event.

That "other Ellen" gave us a joyful year and left another gaping hole in our family. The Ellen exchange had been a big success.

Update: Ellen Beccer became a nurse. When our Ellen married Chris La Shorne in 1981, she and my old friend Bodil came to the wedding, bringing Tron Brandvold, Ellen's fiancé. While she was with us, she bought a wedding gown for herself, the very same model worn by Julie Nixon.

Eventually she became head nurse at an Oslo hospital. She has two children, a boy and a girl, and she continues to live her life with joyful zest.

Reach Out and Touch Someone

The letter began:

> *The first day of July was a very happy day for me. I received a message from AFS (American Field Service) that a host family was found for me in the USA . . . You look like a cozy family. I look forward to meeting you at the end of August.*
>
> *Yours sincerely,*
> *Robin Ringstad*

I had first seen a picture of him only a few weeks earlier. He was a tall young fellow who had lived his whole life on a small island called Vestvågøy, about a hundred miles north of the Arctic Circle, in the Lofoten Islands. His hometown, Leknes, had about one thousand inhabitants. His father had a good job with the public telephone company, but they didn't have a car.

A friend who was a member of the American Field Service had called me, frantic to place Robin. She had run out of families. I offered to help.

Robin described himself as an ordinary boy with a good sense of humor and a love of soccer. The AFS screening committee described him as calm, balanced, mature, and independent. So I made a list of acquaintances who might agree to host an eighteen-year-old boy for the school year and started calling.

Robin arrives.

Two days later I said to my husband, "What do you think about having that Norwegian stay here? He seems like a nice kid." We had four kids out of the house at universities, and the place felt empty. And he's an agreeable man. So of course he left it up to me.

I redecorated a daughter's room, adding some masculine colors and drapes, and I stuck the frilly prom dresses in a closet in another room.

Meanwhile, more letters arrived from Robin. Should he bring a dark suit? (He didn't have one!) How cold would a Chicago winter be? Did we have any travel tips?

Then the August day arrived and he was dropped off in a schoolyard by a bus carrying foreign students who would all be staying in the Chicago area. It was ninety degrees plus, a sharp change from his cool island home. As we drove home, I asked him if the area looked like what he had expected.

After a while he said, "I didn't expect so many trees. Everything is so green."

Soon he was installed in a high school of almost two thousand students, quite a change from his own, with 150 students. He became the star of the soccer team, studied hard, and made good grades. He did his homework lying on his stomach in front of the record player. He ate. And ate. Before the year was over, he had gained twenty-five pounds and grown several inches.

With permission from the high school, he went to work in the biology department at Argonne National Laboratory once a week. Later, he worked for a veterinarian in Iowa for two weeks.

For the first time he saw museums, galleries, a zoo, the Ringling Brothers' Circus, and, of course, the skyline of Chicago. At Easter he drove to Florida with his college sisters, a happy change from the cold winter.

He was used to a very different climate. The Gulf Stream washing up the Norwegian coast makes the islands temperate despite the far north latitude. I had warned Robin that Chicago would be colder than anywhere he had experienced, but he didn't quite believe me until winter struck. At Christmas, all his gifts had to do with being warm! He received a down jacket, scarf, gloves, long underwear, and lined boots.

If he was homesick, we never knew it. In the spring he took a pretty girl to the school dance, and at the award dinner, he was honored for his participation on the soccer team.

Finally it was time to rent a tuxedo and order flowers for the prom. By then he was an all-American kid, bigger in size and maturity. Yet he was still the sensitive, sweet boy from the small Norwegian island. We packed him up and took him to the bus. None of us wanted to cry, but all of us did.

He disappeared onto the bus, sporting a tall Texas hat and a deep suntan.

Update: Robin is in his late thirties now. He's married to his high school sweetheart, Inger, and he has a family of three boys and a girl. He completed his education in Oslo, and, encouraged by his internship experiences in Illinois and Iowa, he became a veterinarian. He lives again in those far northern rocky islands of Lofoten. We share our lives through long newsy letters. We are happy that we opened our home and hearts to Robin; he has paid us back in full measure.

Robin departs.

Get a Grip

Bo Rasmussen was our third and last exchange student. He seemed to roll off the plane, swinging his fisherman's cap in the air, looking like a younger version of John Denver, with long, straight blond hair and steel-rimmed glasses. As I watched him through the windows in the international terminal at O'Hare, I had a gut feeling that this was not to be an easy year, but I'm an optimist.

There had been no AFS pre-screening or letters from teachers and parents. I knew that Bo was fifteen and that his parents ran the local sports and meeting hall in Fjelstrup. They had a house right across the street from my parents and I had seen and met him and his parents many times. They were a friendly people and caring neighbors to my elderly parents, but I was familiar with Bo's "free spirit." When he wrote to ask about taking a break in his schooling in order to visit us from August to April, I could only write back to say that of course he should come.

I wasn't exactly reassured by his mother's letters. She seemed to be worried about him, and she said that she hoped that he would be respectful and considerate, as they had taught him. "Bo seems to think only of himself these days," she lamented.

It didn't take a day to discover that Bo was determined to fit *us* into *his* ideas about lifestyle. Obviously, he had come to the States expecting more freedom. He was shocked to discover that he could not drink beer until age eighteen, a full three years away, and furthermore, that he could not smoke any

We celebrate Bo's birthday.

DG curfew hours

For the information of parents and teenagers, the following is the Curfew Law in Downers Grove.

Curfew hours apply to persons 17 years of age and younger.

The curfew Sunday night through Thursday night is 11 p.m.

Friday and Saturday night curfew time is 12 midnight. Curfew on all days extends to 6 a.m.

Exceptions include when the child is accompanied by a parent, guardian or other adult condoned by a parent or guardian, age 21 or older; and, if the person is engaged in lawful employment only when going directly to or from work.

It is unlawful for a parent or guardian to knowingly allow a child to violate the curfew law.

Fines for violation of curfew are not less than $10 or more than $100.

of the tobacco he had brought with him. And then there was curfew. And homework.

"I came to have fun," he complained.

The answer was simple. "Well then, I hope you have fun doing homework." We explained that in our family, kids were expected to work hard in school, and that while he was with us, he was considered our son.

I called the Dean of Curriculum and forewarned him that he should keep our new kid busy. A smart boy with a high GPA, he was immediately put into honors classes and signed up for soccer. He wrestled and strained and whined like a young wild horse put in harness. He was benched a few times for his smart mouth. He complained about his teachers. Yet he was no quitter, and in the end his pride kept him at it. He saw the names of his friends on the honor roll first grading period, and I explained just what that meant. I said that if he made the honor roll next period, I would be proud to send the clipping to his parents, and that turned out to be the motivation he needed.

Like all of our youngsters, he loved to talk. All of them liked to find me at my desk and drape themselves over a chair or on the carpet for some gabbing. Bo was no exception. He liked to make observations about our family relationships and our family philosophies. When he gave me an opening, talking about trust, I turned to face him and said, "Bo, let's talk about that a bit. I hope you don't think I'm so stupid that I don't know you are smoking pot at school." He was taken by surprise. "Gee, Mom," he said, "you make me feel bad."

"You don't make me feel too great, either," I replied. I explained that how he behaved himself was important to me, especially because he was Danish, and I'm very proud of my country. "Think of it," I said. "You might be the only Dane a lot of these people will ever know." We discussed that for a while and the moment passed. He needed time to digest the conversation and turn it over in his mind.

He never seemed to stop testing us. He didn't think he should follow our rules; he had been making his own for a long time. If he wanted to stay out on those long Danish summer nights, he did. He didn't think his parents had any say-so. Not surprisingly, he behaved the same way at our house, but we weren't going to accept it. We warned him that the town curfew was serious, and that if he got into trouble, he wasn't in a small town in the old country; he was in Downers Grove, Illinois, U.S.A., and he couldn't call his parents to get him out of trouble. But talk was nothing to Bo. The showdown came on a night when he appeared at the front door at 2:30 A.M. drunk on beer.

I came down the stairs like the descent of doom on him, an irate mother in a blue robe. It wasn't easy to get up that much steam at such an hour, but I had been mentally rehearsing it for hours, and what I said—I leave it to the reader's imagination—sobered him up in record time.

The next morning was a Sunday, and I cooked a big breakfast. Bo appeared in his pajamas and I offered him some food. "I can't eat, Mom," he said. "I wrote you a letter. I feel very bad." And he shuffled back to bed.

I sat down on my kitchen stool to read this heart-rending letter from a terribly young boy who knew he had gone too far.

"You've done so much for me and I have been so bad and critical and stupid," he wrote. He lamented his arrogance, poor judgment, and lack of gratitude. "I hope we can be friends again," he went on. "I apologize." After his signature, just "Bo," he added, "Please can I stay until Christmas?"

A few days later we found ourselves in the kitchen at the same time, and I suggested that we try to work things out, like good Danes. We hashed things out for an hour—his side, my side—and we agreed that he would follow our rules and we would keep him until spring as we had planned. He would make us and his parents proud by showing us all that he had what it takes. We shook hands, hugged, and found that we had cleared the air.

One of our points was brought home in a rather scary manner. We had warned him that this was not a small Danish village, and he had to clear his activities and contacts with us. One day while shopping at a photo store, he talked to a man who offered him a job developing pictures in his basement lab. Bo gave him our number, and when he called, I insisted that before Bo could go, we had to have his name and address. After a few calls, I spoke with the man and said that I would bring the boy and pick him up.

"I live so close, that's not necessary, I can be there in a few minutes," the man said. I pressed the matter, and finally he said maybe another time would be better. That was the last of him.

By sheer coincidence I had to take John to a doctor's appointment that evening. I remember vividly how Bo threw the door open as we drove into the garage on our return. His face was full of fear.

He told me that as he was watching TV, a newscast had come on about a fellow called John Wayne Gacy, who had killed and buried a lot of boys in his basement. He realized that he knew nothing about the man who wanted him to go into *his* basement, and that our warnings were not unfounded. It made a profound impression on him.

Still, his adventurous spirit prevailed, and he and a buddy planned a spring break trip by Greyhound bus. They wanted to tour the western United States. I had him write his parents for permission.

He had greatly underestimated the size of this huge country, and after his buddy Tim had his money stolen in a bus station and had to turn back, his sense of adventure was wearing thin. But he stuck it out and came home safely.

Before long it was time for him to go home. He was leaving before the end of our school semester because he had to take some tests for his fall term in Denmark. He packed up his gifts and clothes, and his unused tobacco and pipes, and said his good-byes at school. On one of his last days, we spent the day together, he and I, in Chicago. We took a boat ride and ate a very long lunch at D.B. Kaplan in the Water Tower. We were friends. We had passed the test and both of us had won.

On his day of departure, though, he made one last show of gutsy independence. He put on a very old suit he had inherited from his grandfather! As I watched him climb the stairs of the 747, I knew that Bo had won a piece of my heart.

Update: After Bo finished high school, he became a student sailor on a Danish tall ship named *George Stage* for a year. He talked one of the best shipbuilders in Denmark into taking him on as a pupil, no easy feat.

He worked for another shipbuilder and helped build a catamaran. He crewed on it in races in the North Sea. He bought one of the oldest houses in Fjelstrup and, with the help of a fellow sailor and his sister, totally rebuilt it while he ran a woodworking shop on the same property. He found a nice girlfriend, and last I heard, he was back in school studying international economy. He lives on his boat in the harbor of the town of Årbus with his girlfriend, Hanne. He also staged an art show of his own paintings and wood sculptures.

We hear from him sporadically. During my many trips to Denmark, he has never failed to come and see me. He shows his love and affection for our whole family and his appreciation for the part we played in his struggle toward maturity. The changes that took place in him during that year away from home prompted his father to remark, "I don't know what happened to our son while he was there, but when he came back, he acted

as though he really liked us."

That was a good reward for the struggle.

After Bo, we stopped importing kids. I got a job selling Scandinavian furniture and began to look forward to new adventures.

Bo on his boat, 2000.

The In-Between Years

After we saw Bo, our last imported student, disappear into the jet plane a wiser, stronger young person, Jake and I set forth to expand our world and become wiser and stronger and more diversified ourselves.

We signed up for classes at the junior college and picked up computer skills—writing classes for me, wine-making for Jake—and let us not forget square dancing!

Meanwhile our family expanded in many directions. We welcomed new family members, sons-in-law and a daughter-in-law and their families. There were graduations, engagements, and three weddings within fifteen months. And eventually our children brought forth little ones. Nine within eight years—five girls and four boys.

I dutifully recorded the changes in our yearly newsletter. As I write these words, five of those grandchildren are away at college, and their parents—our kids—now have empty bedrooms in their houses and they are facing the same kinds of changes in their lives. I marvel over both the predictable and the unpredictable in life—happiness and gratitude blended with fear and uncertainty.

Jake and I became the elder generation as our parents and older family members passed away, and those later years in many ways became the best for us.

Even with the kids spread out over many states, we managed to maintain the family unit. The empty beds were regularly filled by our visiting children and guests from many lands. We gathered for reunions, the most memorable being the day our children sent us away and somehow begged and borrowed tables and chairs

We enjoyed our surprise tenth anniversary party.

The cake at our tenth anniversary party sustained just a little bit of dog damage.

and grills so that on our return we were greeted by about seventy friends and relatives who had come to celebrate our tenth anniversary. The dogs took a chunk out of the fancy wedding cake they had bought, but they turned it around, and no one was the wiser.

We called our family together for trips, cruises on fancy boats, and a stay at a dude ranch in the lowlands of Texas. When I was again back on the school bench after one of our gatherings, I put my feelings and impression on paper.

And Then We Were Twenty

Summer, 1996. We were on a cruise ship steaming away from the Florida shore. We had pulled two big round tables together to seat nineteen people. Everyone was dressed up in nice outfits with clean faces and bright smiles. With the adults and their mates were nine bright-eyed children ranging in age from six to fourteen. Only our son John could not be with us.

We raised our glasses of champagne (the children had alcohol-free bubbly supplied by our travel agent!). Jake, also known as Grandpa or Papa, toasted them all and welcomed them aboard for our first floating reunion. His eyes filled with tears of pride, and his voice thickened a bit. His happiness was obvious. This was the first of our four days together on *The Big Red Boat*. Four precious days, each like a fragile moment we knew would end too soon.

We made every hour count. We shared our meals, and of course our memories and laughter. When we reached land at Nassau, we rolled in the waves on the beach. We snorkeled, peeking at the colorful world underwater. Some sailed through the air tied to a big balloon, and the three little ones gathered shells and stones washed up by the sea. Back on the ship, some gambled. Some strolled on deck. Some soaked in the hot tubs. We bought crazy hats and gaudy T-shirts, and the girls had their hair

Aboard the Big Red Boat.

braided with colorful beads at the end. Every night, we gathered at the tables to share our lives.

Twenty-seven years earlier Jake and I, both widowed, had met and married. We had put our lives back together around a big table, melding such different backgrounds and two religions. The years had passed so fast. We looked back on rusty cars driven by teens, and partings for college, weddings and then the precious babies. In time we outgrew our big round family table and added folding tables for holiday feasts. The families spread out over four states from Maryland to Texas, and Jake and I made our visits by plane. Each family began its own traditions around their own tables, and we watched them take root in their own communities. But for four precious days on that ship, we mingled and mixed around two round tables. The chorus of happy voices was the most beautiful sound I've ever heard.

A year later I called the whole family together to celebrate Jake's seventy-fifth birthday and spent the hours between classes at school concocting this poem in his honor:

The Story of Jake: Day by Day

(To Jake from Solveig, April 4, 1997)

How do I start this story of Jake,
of getting together
and pulling up stakes
which brought us all here
on this special day
to celebrate him
who is loved so well.
So much to tell
in so little time

let's take it day by day,
just let it grow
into weeks and months
in one easy flow.

We'll begin
with February 8th in '68,
when Jake worked up the nerve
to re-enter the singles world.
It wasn't easy,
but it was his luck,
to be met by the door
by this brand new greeter
elected just the week before.

"Hello," I said, right friendly-like,
"please sign your name,
come meet the group."
"Welcome," they said.
"Don't you worry—
we've all felt the same
as you do tonight."
We chatted a while
and went to sit
to hear the speech
planned for the meet.

He drank his coffee;
before he left,
"Come back soon," everyone said.
We met again
as the weeks went by.
But on April four
he called for a date.
"It's my birthday"
he quietly said,
"I hoped you would help me celebrate."

But, there was a problem,
I was later told,
the stuff in his closet
was very old.
Off to Herbert's on Main
to get all spruced up.
New jacket and pants,
new shirt and tie,
new socks and new shoes,
to use his own word,
he got himself OYISGEPITZED!!!!
[old Jewish term]
"I had to do something,"
he went on to say,
"I just couldn't be seen
with frayed collars and scuffed shoes
when escorting out
A fancy broad like you!!!"

Well, we talked over dinner,
we talked in the car,
we talked on the phone.
At the kitchen table
with wine and cheese
(and small red radishes)
we shared our past,
our hope and dreams.
Like it's said in the song
"Getting to know you,
getting to know all about you,"
—in record time!

Now you may wonder
what comes next,
I didn't know,
neither did Jake
smart as he was with his Ph.D.

We needed advice,
counsel and help
from somebody smart
with good common sense,
objective wisdom,
that's what we need,
on that we certainly both agreed.

Like a flashbulb
bright in the night
we found the answer
we knew was just right.
Let's ask the kids,
Yeah, that's it,
they will tell us for sure,
with honest thought
and true conviction,
if it is possible for us
to be together
forevermore.

In separate houses
discussions went on,
six kids mulling over,
what had to be done,
with two old people,
who have fallen in love.
"We might as well let them marry,"
they seem to agree,
"It really make sense
that we live in one place
like a real family."

The verdict came down:
"IN FAVOR" they said;
true happiness
suddenly reigned.

Small John, ecstatic,
ran through the house,
hopping and skipping,
yelling out loud,
"We're getting married,
we're getting married,"
his world was complete,
a new brother,
a new sister,
but best of all,
he, like the boys in the street
would have a DAD of his own.

But—
how, what, when, where,
decisions, decisions,
where to begin.
(small miracle brewing)

By August 10,
all had been done,
Two households of things
stuffed into one,
two set of dishes
two vacuums
two irons
two of every little thing
even two dogs
was part of the bargain.

We all got dressed
and went to the church.
Pastor Cook had us sign
on the dotted line,
and when it was done,

and there was no more,
Jake said, "I think I will go
to the hardware store !!!
We all started living
in the big new house
two sets of people
from different faiths
from different lives
but very intent
on pulling together
as a family of eight.

So, now you see
how very important
a birthday can be.
After that first call on the phone
Jake has never again been alone.
We all love him
and wish him well
and that's all of the story
I have time to tell.

In between family get-togethers, Jake and I found time to roam the world. We sailed the calm waters of the South Pacific on a small freighter that touched land on small, sparsely inhabited islands. We watched giraffes trying to touch the African sky and elephants herding and protecting their young while lions lay hidden in the grass. We climbed the great wall in China, and we stood humbly by the Holy Wall in Jerusalem. Fearfully we crossed the Berlin Wall after getting lost on the wrong side on a rainy day. In Venezuela we encountered yet another wall. This one, topped with shards of glass, surrounded my sister and her stately family home, and dogs patrolled her gardens.

These walls left an unexpected impression on me, and I found myself putting words and feelings on paper when I returned to my writing classes.

The Purpose of Walls

On one of our many travel expeditions, my husband and I finally stood at the Great Wall of China. It is known as one of the seven wonders of the world; indeed, it can be seen by astronauts sailing through outer space. It is awesome, colossal, monumental! We started climbing some of the thousand high and strenuous steps, but rather than feeling a sense of awe, humility, or whatever one is supposed to feel, I found myself getting angrier and more irritated at each step. My friends and fellow travelers, while huffing and puffing, exclaimed that it was impressive, mind-boggling, fantastic, etc. I nodded in agreement, all the while trying to identify what I was getting so disgruntled about.

We reached a high point—a lookout platform, so to speak. We could indeed see the Wall for miles and miles, resembling a giant snake slithering across the landscape. For miles and miles it went on, turning and twisting into the horizon. Solid and forbidding, with brutal strength, it dominated the mountainous, barren landscape. One could not help looking at it—I guess "riveting" is the word I am looking for. It was indeed just that.

It was not until we were back in our hotel and I was lying on my bed that I began to identify the anger I had felt while stomping up that ugly wall. Strangely enough, a kindly, sensitive man in our group had said to me, as we reentered the bus, "Solveig, did I say anything wrong up there on the wall, something which upset you?" "No, no," I assured him. "Why in the world would I be upset with you?" It seemed he had said something or other as we passed each other on our climb and I had turned and given him an angry glare. Was my face such a reflection of feelings that I had not even identified myself?

However, as I lay on my bed hours later, the Wall, and all the other walls I had seen before, came back on my horizon. The China wall that I had just walked on, the Berlin wall painted with defiant graffiti, where we could see soldiers pointing guns at us from the Russian side, the walls surrounding countless castles I had seen in many countries including my homeland, Denmark.

Even the wall around my sister's house in Venezuela. What purpose do walls serve—what do they signify?

All I can think of is that they signify one man's power over others. Man has a need to amass a great deal of material goods, so much that he has to build a wall around it to protect it—and in doing so, he himself becomes a prisoner inside of it. My sister lives in a house so large and elegant, with so many riches and costly belongings, that it has to be protected not only with a wall with shards of glass on top and a strong, double-locked iron gate, but also with two fierce German shepherds patrolling the grounds.

One can also build walls around oneself and most likely end up being lonely and isolated from the rest of the world.

China's wall was ordered to be built by one man, the emperor, who had power over millions of men. The purpose was to keep the enemy away from his land. The endless supply of manpower nullified the pain and suffering of the individual souls. There were always more men—an unending supply, replaced by new generations.

The Berlin wall was built to keep people from escaping a government that was forced on them. Both the Chinese wall and the German wall outgrew their purposes.

My husband was convinced—absolutely sure—that the Berlin wall would stand forever and that Germany would never be reunited. As sure as he was that he was right, I was just as sure that he was not!

Nothing is permanent—not the Berlin wall or the Great Wall of China. Eventually it, too, will crumble. It has occurred to me that in spending these years writing the life stories of my parents and of my own childhood and youth, I am making an attempt to break down the barriers—walls, one may say—between our generations. I try to let my children and their children get a glimpse into my world and to let them see me, not only with my white hair and aging body, but as I lived and worked when I was their age.

To say it simply, I am trying to break down the walls and help them across the rubble so our hands and minds can meet.

As I finish this chapter in 2004, another wall is being built in Israel by the Jewish people. Only history will tell if it will help them to keep peace in the sparse piece of land they were given some fifty years ago.

But our families were free—not fettered by walls. Our children were free to be educated, to pick their professions, to gather and communicate.

When we were all together, we did sing and laugh with joy and happiness. But in that perfect world, something was still amiss.

Our son, John, now with a strong, lanky 6-foot-3 body and handsome face, was hindered by a few misplaced brain cells that I first noticed in his infancy. It didn't show: his voice and eyes were clear. He could read and write and speak intelligently, but he could not find his destiny or control his life.

His story is the last to be told in my series of seven. He flavored our lives, but he did not diminish our love.

This page: In the wilds of Africa and at the Great Wall of China.

Opposite: The freightboat Aranui *in the South Seas.*

Good-bye to Jake

My year-end newsletters halted in 2002.

The spring and summer months of that year were filled with our usual activities. Friends flled our garden for the Fourth of July picnic. Kids came and went, and Jake joined me at the Iowa Writing Festival. He went to the lab most days and still carried his basketball in the backseat of the car for his respites at the YMCA. He continued to collaborate with some of his old colleagues on a book about the old days of the A-bomb project; and he steadily checked on the many gallons of wine brewing in our basement.

But as the months wound down into fall, he began to need an extra lamp to read his morning newspaper. After a quick overnight meeting with his buddies in Atlanta, he finally saw the eye doctor.

Our calendar began to fill with doctor visits, tests, hospitalizations, and finally a nursing home stay. The small, painless tumor that grew in Jake's brain took away his sight, it took away his strength, but it did not take away his will.

Together we battled this unseen foe. But within five months he closed his eyes and went away.

Our thirty-five years together was a true love story. We held onto each other during good times and bad. He was the true treasure of my seven lives.

Jake Sedlet
April 4, 1922–March 29, 2003

For Jake

I held him in my arms
the words had all been said
the room was still
but for the humming fan
on the windowsill
We heard the music play
we held hands
as we always had
our brains in rhythm
going over things
of memories
of life and love
of ups and downs
of places near and far
let's go and see the kids
I wonder how they are
and the little ones
how fast they grew
they learned to walk and read
and talk on the telephone
We didn't need the words
just touching was enough.
You are still my sweetheart
I told him
You bet, he softly said.

7

JOHN
A Troubled Soul

John Walking

My boy is walking in the street. The wind blows the snow until it forms waves across the lawn, creeping into every crack and seam.

I see him there, away from shelter, under the sky that hangs over him like a frozen, sunless wall. He walks in his own lonely world, his head turned down, his feet dragging the icy burden on his boots.

Once I held his small, warm body close to me, looked into his smiling eyes, felt his small hand grasp my finger.

He grew, he stumbled and reached out for help, but my arms were not long enough; my love was not big enough; the help I could find was not good enough.

Slowly, subtly, a few brain cells became the power and the distance, separating him from me, his world from mine. The distance grew into a chasm and I could not reach him. I could only cry out: *Is he forever lost? Will he ever heal?*

Will I ever again see his smiling eyes looking into mine?

Childhood

When my loving husband, Ray, died suddenly and tragically, I was left with my three beautiful daughters and a four-month-old son, John. All my life I had been taught, had learned, and had practiced my mother's wisdom: see what needs doing, and start doing it. Even in the midst of great sorrow, a mother has to gather her wits and go on. My children were my blessing.

John was a special one for all of us. Born six years after his youngest sister, he was a beautiful, well-formed child who gave us much pleasure with his sweet temper, his curiosity, the quickness of his hazel-green eyes, his ready smile. I don't know what my nights would have been like after Ray's death without him, because as I sat up through many lonely winter vigils, I had this child to feed and rock. I knew I would have God's help.

All my adult life, I had been involved with children, starting with my special pediatric training in my late teen years. Looking back from John's later years, I remembered that early on there were small things that struck me as odd in his behavior and his development, but they were, truly, small: talking late (like Einstein!); his distractibility; his resistance to any kind of confinement. I remember how, when he was placed in a baby seat, he would often arch his back so that only the back of his head and his heels touched the seat. If he was placed in a playpen he cried pitifully, no matter what toys we gave him or how close by I and his sisters were.

I voiced some of my concerns to our pediatrician and asked her to check John's hearing. She was indulgent with me (or condescending?), rapping instruments to make a bell-like sound to get John's attention and turning to tell me that he could hear just fine. I recall that he reached for her French-rolled hair, and she gently told him no, then turned to tell me he was perfect. So I told myself she knew best.

Yet this small child, sitting in his high chair, would sometimes become so entranced that I could not get a reaction with my voice or a wave of my hand in front of his eyes. I took comfort from seeing how he was thriving, eating well, enjoying his food, even humming and uttering sounds of pleasure at morsels he liked.

As he began to move about, I bought a little scooter called, I believe, a Kiddy Cart, and he learned to maneuver it skillfully through the house, speeding past furniture and through the doorways. We were living in the old house my husband and I had bought in Downers Grove, and the floors tilted slightly downward into the kitchen. I can still see this little bundle of energy propelling himself through the family room, living room, and dining room, gathering speed as he arrived in the kitchen with its slanting floor. It always seemed that he must crash against the cabinet doors, but without fail he used his heels as brakes and stopped within an inch of the obstacle, grinning from ear to ear. We, of course, sprang out of his way in the nick of time, clapping our hands in admiration. He would then turn the cart around and return by the same route, panting and drooling all the while.

He seemed to have complete trust in the world. He was never afraid of new people or new sounds. I remember Pastor Johnson from the Congregational Church, who had baptized and welcomed this little person into the church family, and who a few months later bade his father farewell and helped me escort him to his resting place. As the pastor sat talking to me, he looked at John and said, "Does that baby ever cry? I've never heard him cry."

My response was, "Why should he cry? The whole world around him loves him so much he has no reason to cry!"

The first time anyone other than I took notice of my small son's possible difference was when he was three years old, attending a church preschool program. At a conference, the director of the school gently mentioned her concern. "Solveig," she said, "you must watch out for John. You may have some problems." She tried, at the same time, to reassure me, but I already knew, or suspected, that she was right.

Kindergarten came and John went through it twice. He wasn't ready for first grade, they told me. After first grade the school psychologist advised us to take him in for a brain scan. We made an appointment at Northwestern University Hospital with a Dr. Boshes, who, we were told, was the best in the field of child neurology.

The Good Doctor

By the time we visited Dr. Boshes, I had been widowed five years and had met and married Jake Sedlet and joined my family with him and his two children, Steve and Susan. John was thrilled to have a father at last, like

Uncle John with Paul and John.

his friends. Indeed, he had often asked me to go and get him a dad. He thought I should "go to a Daddy Store and pick one out"! He wondered if God could fix up his daddy and send him back, or if he could see him if he climbed the tallest tree in our yard.

Jake and I were one year into our marriage as we headed off to the famous Dr. Boshes. We were most awed and respectful, and anxious not to interfere with the examination, so we stood away from the table where John was seated. I was at the end of the room, and Jake was in the doorway. We watched as the doctor told John to wag his tongue from side to side, to touch his nose with his forefinger while his eyes were closed, and so on. John seemed to enjoy all of the exercises as if they were games. We filled out forms and made an appointment for a brain scan the next day.

John and I returned the next morning. Electrodes were pasted to his head. He didn't object, but when he was given a sleep medication so that the scan would show his brain at rest, he did not fall asleep. He was given a second dose, and this dear, cooperative little boy became a restless, uncontrollable small animal. It was impossible to get a sleep pattern, and the technician sent us away.

Little John, Big John, and Jamie

I drove us home in heavy rush hour traffic with great difficulty, as I could not control John while minding the driving. He seemed to be flying from one side of the car to the other. We were in a long three-seat station wagon. He crawled from one end to the other, over the backs of seats, onto the floor and back up. Fortunately, all the doors could be locked from the front panel. When we reached the house he stormed through it. It took hours for him to settle down. Jake had to put chairs in front of the fireplace to keep him from running straight into it. Even when we finally got him to bed, he slept fitfully, waking often, though he did not cry.

When we went back to Dr. Boshes for the follow-up visit, all of us were seated in his office. He glanced at John's chart and said, "It seems like all went well and your boy will be fine, what with the good school system in your town. He has some minor brain dysfunction, but his brain scan shows no serious problem, nor did the exam that I did with him in my office here."

This news, of course, delighted us—except that I was uneasy about the fact that John didn't go to sleep during the test. When I mentioned that, the good doctor, for reasons I will never understand, reminded me irritably that *he* was the doctor and he knew how to read charts. He became angrier as he spoke. He said he had observed that I was a remote,

uncaring mother, and that Jake was more like a grandfather than a father; he said that if John continued to live without love and affection, he would have a most worrisome future! When I tried to assure him that John was the dearest, most beloved little child you could find, he became utterly incensed with me. He stood up, told me that he was not there to argue with us, and he saw no reason to continue the visit.

We had a grim ride back to Downers Grove.

I realize now that the first awful seeds of guilt and fear were sown right then, right there, in that doctor's office. I was to be haunted by his judgment for many years to come.

Your child starts to slip away from you in ways that you do not understand. You love him with all your heart, and you give him all the security, warmth, and opportunities available to you—the same ones, or more, that you gave his sisters—and *it isn't enough*. Maybe the girls were just lucky! Maybe your misjudgment has caught up with you!

New friends tell me that even now, when doctors know much more, and information is available to the public more readily, parents, especially mothers, are sometimes made to feel responsible, and therefore guilty, for their children's psychological problems. If you are careful and watch-

ful and attentive, you are a smothering mother. If you encourage independence and provide opportunities for your children to make their own mistakes and learn consequences, you are an uncaring, remote mother. If you step back and let the doctors take over, you are absconding from your duties. If you stay close and ask questions and try to understand everything that is going on with your child, you are interfering.

I can't explain these things, and I hope there are many exceptions—situations where parents are involved in ways that support them and inform them—but I do know this: If I had not fought like a tiger for my son, year after year, he would be probably be dead by now. It took years for him to receive the help he needed, and it did not come knocking at our door. This pushy mother went looking.

But on that ride home from Dr. Boshes' office, I was so overwhelmed with sadness, still mourning my dead husband, now stunned by accusations about my mothering, that I could do nothing but cry. Delayed grief? Fear and foreboding? I don't know. I just know I could not stop the flood of tears.

Jake, who was a wonderfully kind man, tried to reassure me, to calm and soothe my obvious pain, but tears burned my eyes and blurred my vision. The seeds sown that day eventually grew into a bramble so large and thick we could not see beyond it. Its roots infiltrated our family and clogged our communication lines with confusion, fear, and sorrow.

There would be many more tears before I found my strength and John learned how to make a life.

A Long History

Life goes on. As John progressed through grade school, we continued to seek advice and assistance. There were repeated staffings with the school psychologist about John's inability to cooperate with teachers and to interact with his peers except for his one close friend and neighbor, Jamie. He had problems with anything that required follow-through, like take-home assignments, etc., but he was not disruptive or impolite. We were visited by a school-assigned social worker who pronounced us secure and stable and loving, a pleasant relief that did not, of course, help solve our problems.

Jake was on the school board for six years and also joined Indian Guides, attending meetings and camping expeditions with John. I threw myself into many school activities, including volunteering for the "picture lady" program, and being a room mother, den mother, and Sunday School teacher in John's room, trying, unsuccessfully, to get him to go. One summer we spent $1200 to get him into an Elmhurst College reading program, with little gain. His stepbrother, Steven, took him spelunking, and he did like that.

John had a rich family and neighborhood life with his siblings, friends, and pets. Our surroundings were wonderful for a child, with a nearby pool, a farm, and even a big mud hole at the end of the street. (He called it the "digging place.") He loved outings, camping trips, and visits to relatives in Denmark and Florida. He seemed to enjoy being the youngest, and he was affectionate. He had a hard time with even small chores, though, and occasionally he expressed jealousy, but he seemed to be growing well both physically and emotionally. I tried to believe school was hard for him and that as he matured he would improve. The opposite proved to be true.

In junior high school there were numerous conferences as we all tried to guide him into classes and activities that would challenge him (just enough), interest him (fully), and hold his attention over time. He joined band, playing clarinet, and did well, then lost interest and quit after the first year. He attended a Boy Scout camp with his dad, but didn't interact with other kids. Later, he spent seven weeks at Camp Algonquin in Rhinelander, Wisconsin, a reading camp, where he caused no real problems, but also did not really accomplish much.

John's graduation from junior high school, with Karen and Ellen.

226

By high school he was being placed in Special Education classes, mostly because of his difficulty with social skills. He couldn't keep up with his classmates. He tried the swim team, at the coach's invitation, and a scuba class, but his inability to stick with things—and his growing fears—began to emerge and overwhelm him. He switched to trade school but didn't do well there either, in the print shop activities he had chosen. Despite all of our best efforts, our sunny little boy was becoming an angry young man. Yet he was able to visit a former exchange student in Norway the summer after his junior year and seemed to get along fine.

During his senior year, he didn't so much attend school as roam the school hallways. He tried to work part-time, first as a busboy, later in a kennel, but his defiant attitude got him fired. He did graduate, in June 1982, and he was determined to join the army. He had to wait until fall, and the atmosphere in our home through the summer was tense as he grew disrespectful and verbally abusive. He had such a row with Ellen, who had a baby by then, that the police were called.

He did join the army, but in no time he was calling for help. We kept saying, "Hang tough. Talk to the chaplain. Solve your own problems."

John with Mom and Dad on high school graduation day.

In seven weeks he was home. The army said he could try again in two years. I met him at the airport: a dirty, unwashed, sad, sobbing boy in a gangly man's body. Jake was kind to him, but none of us knew quite how to help. We urged him to find a holiday job.

He worked for Toys 'R' Us during Christmas, and then Ellen helped him to get a job at Presbyterian St. Luke's Hospital in Chicago as a delivery person for the Central Pharmacy. It was a good job, though unsurprisingly, he was a loner socially.

He began to see a psychiatrist, Dr. Nyquist, in Hinsdale, and all sorts of new reviews occurred, from scholastic aptitude for John to family history for the rest of us. Of course, none of it was considered "our business," and at any rate, John soon decided soon after that he didn't want to see the doctor any more.

He kept his job into spring and then asked for a counselor again. I found him Dr. Hill in Elmhurst, and I also took him to the YMCA in La Grange so that he could see how well-equipped and friendly a place it was. It had a residence, too, so he moved in that summer of 1983, when he was twenty, and soon made friends with a young man named Keith, who turned him on to beer and drugs.

John with nieces and nephews.

Before long the two of them took off for Colorado, and what followed is a kind of litany of repeated troubles: jobs held for a short time; money acquired and spent; John stranded and hitchhiking or walking; tension, anger, grief, depression, rage. He was growing worse.

He could not hold a job. He could not make good decisions about managing the most basic aspects of his life. (For example, he let Keith talk him into taking out his inheritance from an uncle and spending it; then Keith took off.) When things went wrong, he turned to pot or drink, he smashed things, he screamed abuse.

He began to tell us wild stories about being chased by terrible drug dealers, being threatened. He wandered, walking or driving around. He begged for help, then turned on us when we gave it. As an adult, he had the "right" to make his own decisions, and we had no "right" to tell him what to do. All we could do was to offer advice he refused and try to go on with our own lives. We were urged by counselors to keep him out of our house, to let him "hit bottom." Something about that inevitability was supposed to be magical. I don't know how it works for alcoholics and drug addicts, but I can tell you it doesn't work with the mentally ill, maybe because there is no bottom, or because the bottom is where they live.

John was furious and broke a window to get into our house. We gave him money, but then we drew up formal legal papers forbidding him access to our home. I won't even try to describe what this was like for me.

Jake and I had made plans to go to Europe, and we went on with them. While we were gone John slept in his car, used money for drugs, and tried to stay with childhood friends—who could not put up with him. We came back to a kind of siege state, afraid of our own home. Within two hours of our return he turned up, and within two days he went on a rampage at the Y, stealing from others and messing up rooms.

The days that followed our return were a nightmare of police intervention, John's demands and threats, and his actual attacks against Jake. We were afraid of him. I called Madden Mental Health Center and was told that because John was an adult, they could not take him against his will unless he was brought by the police. Yet when the police came out and found him asleep downstairs, they declared him "fine." We asked that he be arrested for trespassing; in the station, he had a tantrum and was booked.

On and on this story goes, with escalating crises, outlays of money, interventions, and pleas with counselors, police, and crisis units for help. There was a period when we lost John and did not hear from him for two months. He ended up in the Wheaton jail for four months, and I went to see him every week. When he was released, we found him a room in Downers Grove, but in no time he was in trouble again. We lived our lives, in the way of one-foot-in-front-of-the-other, but John had made our lives a heap of shards. I could only imagine what it was like for him.

Help at Last

For years, Jake and I blamed ourselves. We could spend entire days saying what we should have done and what we should not have done. We combed every memory, went over every detail. I wrote incessantly, keeping records, listing names, pouring out emotions. This great failure of ours, our John, affected every corner of our lives: our friendships, our family, even our marriage.

I don't think any more about what I might have done differently. I don't think I could have altered the end result. Maybe if I had known more at the beginning we could have reached it sooner; maybe not. I have to remember that we, the parents and the son, we are the "lay" people here. We are the clients, the needy, the seekers. No one should expect us to know everything. The doctors and counselors were the experts. Figure that out.

On the morning after John threatened to kill Jake with his bare hands, a counselor named Winscott interviewed John in his bedroom and then told us, "He's all right! And by the way, you've got a nice home."

Dr. Nyquist put his hand on my shoulder as I wept and said, "Your son can be helped," but he wasn't.

Bernadette Dugan from the DuPage Counseling Service said, "Throw your son out; when he hits the bottom of the trash pile, he will straighten out." I don't know if that had been her experience before, but John was going to take us with him, one way or the other.

"Oh, let him go on with his adventure," said Dr. Hill from Elmhurst when John took all of his money out of the bank, left his good job, and drove to Colorado with Keith.

I've barely mentioned the names here. I have documented all of John's difficulties from kindergarten through high school, class by class: teachers, counselors, school psychologists. No one ever asked me what I thought! They dispersed their knowledge and dismissed our observations.

No one ever considered collaborating with us in serving our son's needs. I have read that in other countries, like Italy and India, families sometimes move in with a sick child, and families, even whole villages, are considered a support system for the mentally ill. Perhaps we have fallen victim to our culture of expertise at the cost of some of our humanity.

Like the hairline cracks in the walls, the small things slowly went askew, and no one saw it coming but us. Yet what did we know? When I tried to say that John's birth father had suffered from depression, and that there had been other cases of mental illness in his family background, no one cared to know.

Jake said, "They are only interested in the present."

I say: They were only interested in their opinions. Their theories. Their fees.

How rich is the irony in what I tell now! That a good man with no fancy degrees, a man who paid attention and cared, a man whose learning was all from experience, came to our rescue.

Jake and I sold our house and fled into a security apartment in Darien, a village near where we had been living. Later we uprooted ourselves again and moved with John to La Crosse, Wisconsin. One night I lay in terror, listening to him curse and howl and snicker and bang the walls in the basement below my room. I didn't lock my door; what good would that do? One good kick would have been enough. Jake was in Illinois finishing up things at the lab. My "self-defense weapon" was a can of hair spray I kept by my pillow. If in his disturbed rage John attacked me, I hoped I could blind him long enough to get away.

Was I frightened? Surely I was, but I wasn't going to abandon my son, and deep in my heart I still believed that God was with me as he had been down all this rocky road we had traveled.

When dawn broke I crept soundlessly to the kitchen, got my car keys, and backed my car into the street for the two-block ride to my daughter Karen's house. The family had just begun to stir when I banged on the front door. When Karen, in her robe, saw my face, she said, "We must call the police!"

"No," I pleaded. "No more police. I'll call John on the phone and try to calm him down."

When I reached him, after only two rings, he answered cheerfully. I told him that we needed help, that he had to see a doctor.

"No, Mom," he said. "I'm fine. Why don't you come home and we'll have a nice breakfast together, just you and me." Under his cheerful tone he was mocking, and then he started to giggle.

We did call the police. The officer came to Karen's house a few minutes later and stood in the doorway talking to us as John came blithely strolling toward the house.

The policeman had the look of a family man. He was near retirement, perhaps in his fifties. He was a calm, friendly, solid man.

"Hi John," he said. "What seems to be the problem?"

"There's no problem, sir," John said. "No problem at all."

"Well, son," the policeman said quietly, "your Mom seems to be very upset. Let's you and me go sit in my car and talk about it."

To our enormous relief, John agreed, and he followed the officer to his squad car.

In about ten minutes (though it seemed forever), the officer came back and told us that John had agreed to go to the hospital.

The officer had no psychology degree. He was a small-town cop. He didn't talk down to John or scold him. He didn't try to intimidate him or use force. He didn't try to make me feel useless, either. He just did the right thing. Was that God's intervention, or just luck? The right man answered our call that morning.

There were more bad times to come, of course: frightening, awful, humiliating times. But the initial intervention of that soft-spoken policeman was the first effective action anyone had taken to set in motion events that would name John's trouble and point him toward help.

My dear son suffers from a severe mental illness called schizophrenia. He isn't a bad person, and neither are his parents. We're all unlucky. He is sick.

Steps toward a Life

The first step in solving a problem is to name it. John's treatment plan at the hospital set down in black and white his delusions and impairments; his anxiety and self-doubt and refusal to work as a result; his abuse of alcohol, drugs and caffeine; his overall failure to develop a suitable way to live in the community.

Until John's problems were identified, there was no place to go with him—nothing to serve as a vessel for our hope. In the hospital, goals were set, medicines were assigned, and eventual transition into the community was planned.

None of these things were easy. He had habits and fears of long duration, and he was used to running from the responsibilities he was certain he could not meet. He was used to calling his mom, plaintive in his need, then brutal in his rejection of advice, and it was a long time before he was able to depend on other people and on himself in meaningful ways. What he had to give up was, in a sense, his freedom; he could not handle a life that was open-ended. He could not make decisions on the fly. The range of his emotions ran from cheerfulness to exasperation to desperation to fury. And, of course, my life was rocked by these emotions, too.

Besides that, we discovered, as we might have expected, that some of those who worked with John had no special interest in what his family had to say, what we knew about him, what our fears for him were. Curiously, considering the situation we found ourselves in, two of my daughters had entered the medical field in their professions, one as a nurse, one as a pharmacist. Sometimes it took all of us to push against the stubbornness of a counselor making a quick decision based on experience—experience with people other than John! I can only think that this kind of work is so difficult that people become detached and stop listening; either that or the wrong kind of people are called to it. When you meet a mental health worker who truly listens, it is a kind of miracle, and it can mean everything to the management of treatment.

He calls on Sundays. "Hello Mom." "Hello John." So it has been for more than twenty years—calls from near and far, in times of trouble and despair, from jail cells, lonely phone booths, or crowded bars in faraway states.

Now the calls are mostly upbeat, peaceful; the voice relaxed. He will say, "I did my laundry this week. I went to Human Services for my meds and money. I worked for Chris (brother-in-law); I had my blood tests. I took the bus to the mall and grocery store. My plants are growing well. My fish are still alive."

His life is regimented: pills at a certain time; counselor visits every week; the psychiatrist once a month. He keeps appointments with a probation officer and a court-appointed psychologist. He visits his friends, Dean and Don.

And on Sunday he calls Mom.

John is over forty now, living in an apartment carved out of a formerly stately house. It has high ceilings, carved woodwork, many windows. He has two large rooms and a bath of his own. It is the best apartment he has ever had. He says it feels like a real home.

He fought moving there vehemently, crying, begging, threatening, and accusing us and his counselor, saying that we were manipulating his mind and forcing him to do things he did not want to do.

He had been living in a completely inadequate situation, but he insisted that the roaches that crept through his walls and ceilings from neighboring apartments did not bother him. His sisters Ellen and Karen recruited their husbands, their friends, and an exterminator to rid the place of the pests. We installed new carpets. Good old Mom came in with buckets, brooms, ammonia, bleach and Lysol. The place smelled like a chemistry lab, but in a couple of weeks the roaches moved back in, and finally John called to say, "I give up in the war on roaches."

We sprang into action. The probation officer and counselor Chad found the apartment. The parents shopped at Salvation Army and Goodwill stores (bless those folks!) and within a week we found John a sofa, kitchen set, TV bench, and an extra-long bed for his extra-long body. His sisters sterilized his belongings and his bags and moved them into storage until all could be moved into this new apartment—this new chapter in his life.

His life now is streamlined. He cooks in a microwave and eats on paper plates with plastic utensils. The stove is unsplattered, and little has to be washed. His life runs smoothly and tension-free most of the time, and his mind is at ease.

On Sundays he tells me how he feels, and sometimes he talks about the past. About life in the streets and in jail cells. He reminisces about different jails as another person might mention travels to other countries. Kane County, he says, was the best. There, the warden gave him a room with a soft bed. The cook, who liked him, gave him large portions to fatten him up. He slept and slept, feeling safe and at peace.

At Wheaton's jail, he asked to be put in isolation to get away from the rowdy inmates in the common shelter. There were inmates in neighboring cells who were condemned to death for a murder they did not do. (Later, in fact, they were exonerated and freed.) He recalls the terror of the Cook County jail, where he hid under the bed until he was transferred into the psychiatric unit. Most humiliating was the La Crosse jail, where he was crowded, four men together, in a small dirty cell that should have held one.

But he says, "I needed to be in jail, Mom. My life was out of control and it kept me away from the bad stuff." He tells me about Dana, a young Bible-stomper who visited him in Wheaton and challenged him to study the Bible. How that stirred his competitive spirit! He read the good book twice and was able to stump even Dana!

All those times, when he was in jail, I visited him every week. I could not touch him, but we could talk through the glass on the phone. Once I arrived to be told that I wasn't yet "on his list," so I could not visit him. I simply fell apart, weeping uncontrollably, until a guard relented in the face of this mother's tears.

✳

If our lives go as they are meant to go, John's will go on beyond my own, but as long as I am here, he is my son, and his pain and confusion have been mine, too. I wish that he had an easier life, of course. I wish that he had his own family and the pleasures of a profession. But the grievousness and struggle of his life have taught all of us in his family lessons of love and struggle that do not come from books. We have learned hard truths about the imperfect world that we thought was quite apart from our own. Oh, I had had hints, in my own family's life and in stories I heard, but this was something else. I know deep in my bones that human nature is frail, that it is wrong to take good things for granted, that even friends are unpredictable, and that experts and professionals and the powerful, for all their intimidation and their arrogance and their advice, are just human, too.

John took this family through dark chambers as we groped our way toward help for him and toward the proper roles for ourselves. We cried fitfully in our helplessness, but ever so slowly, over twenty years' time, we have emerged as a solid family, more united than ever, forever devoted to the young son whose tortured mind took us into the worst we could have imagined could befall us as a family. We weathered it, clinging to faith and to one another; and in time, we drifted into a kind of serenity.

John lives in guarded peace, dependent on people and on medicine and on regimen and on his own will. His years have brought him maturity and insight into his illness, and have made his life bearable. I think that at times he is happy.

A Mother's Poems for her Son

1.

The Question

Onto the pages
flow thoughts
of grief
and joy

Do I need to write?
Do I need to cry?
Do I need to rest
and sleep?

Do I need to wonder?
Do I need to see?
Do I need to listen?
Do I need to be?

My son—
his pleading eyes
his signs of fear—
he begs of me,
Do not go,
I need you here!

Can I save him
and make him well
if I sacrifice myself?

2.

He looks at me,
a familiar face,
a source of love
that never ends.
Mom, oh Mom,
I am glad you came.
Stay with me.
Just sit
and be.

Oh God I love him.
He is my only son.
His body wasted
his hands so thin
his eyes so empty;
mine filled with tears.

I gave him life
yet he is not mine.
He has a purpose
he cannot find.
What is his destiny?
Why must he be?

In his head
are thoughts and voices
no one else can hear
who speak to him.
What must he bear!

Who comforts him?
What can he do?
The voices,
do they tell him?
Do they guide him?
Are they behind
those empty haunting eyes?

In my silent room
so all alone
I yell at God.
I beg for help,
I cry and moan.
Grief and sadness beyond belief.
God please help
my innocent child.

3.

Pleading

There he is, my only son
with the empty pleading eyes,
pain showing
through every body cell
pain confusion questions
more questions
searching for answers
begging for help.

Why am I like this?
Why can't I change?
His eyes plead with me
to give him answers.

He fights he curses
He whimpers and cries.
The comfort I give
does not suffice.

Does God have a plan
for my only son
with the hurting
haunting empty eyes?

Is he God's child
like Jesus?
Must he suffer
like Him
To teach us faith
and humility?

Like Jesus
he begs:
Do not leave me
Hold me
Do not forsake me.
Help me understand
why I am different.
Why did God give me life?

Help him, please God,
Let peace come to him.
Dry away the tears
for him and for me.
Set us free
of pain and doubt.
Give us strength, faith and trust.
Oh God help us understand.

I see him
through the glass
Where they locked him in
to make him obey.
He is caught in a web
and he can never be free.

4.

The Flow of a Life

This is the way
that life begins
from darkness to light,
the babe in the womb.
for that newborn
full of noise and sound,
the eyes unused to light,
but mother's voice,
her skin, her face
holding murmuring
comfort
familiar love.

This is the way
when the bones grow strong
the child walks and runs
he sees and touches
and learns right from wrong.
His world expands
outside that room
outside the home
way down the road
to the big school house
that he enters, Mom at his side
to begin a new day in his life.

The life in the school
lasts years and years.
Mom coaching, accepting his fears.
his world opens
to all new things:
Reading, mathematical skills.
onward, onward he
must follow along.
The years soon pass.
His legs have grown long.
His days at school
soon will be gone.

Yet a new world
is facing him.
He must decide
where he will go,
what he will do.
He cannot run.
He cannot hide.
His Mom can guide him
and give him courage
but his life is his
to face alone.
Such is the way
for that little newborn.

5.

Blurred Vision

I cannot enter your mind.
You live so far from me
I am as frustrated and as
helpless as you.
We live on different planes,
The mystery of brain cells
like a blurred road map,
keeps us from reaching each other.
I want you to conform and
fit yourself into my lifestyle
but you cannot.
You speak to me, you growl
You yell and threaten,
trying to make me understand
your world is different
and so very far from mine.

6.

Acceptance:
A Gift to the Troubled Soul

There is a time
when acceptance comes
like gentle winds
and soothing rain.
It blows away worries,
and cleans the soul.
Old hurts flow away.

Acceptance fills
the body and mind,
brings peace and solace
when all seem lost.
When eyes are blind
the world all dark
bright rays of sun
suddenly
break through
the heavy clouds.

There is a time
to say to oneself
Put your trust in God;
All will be well.